M y name is Leigha Janelle Curry.

On February 14th, 1982, I was born in secret and abandoned by my mother. I have lived forty years without knowing the details of my biological family. Until now.

FOUND AND LOST

A True Story About Determination,
Perseverance, and Faith.

DEDICATION

This book is dedicated to my family, friends, and fellow adoptees.

To my fellow adoptees, you are loved, valued, and definitely not alone. Tell your story and live it out loud.

This is for you!

To my mommy and daddy, I am forever grateful for the love, guidance, and support that you continue to give me. I am who I am because of you. Thank you for never giving up on me. No one will ever understand how much you mean to me. From the smallest gestures to the biggest sacrifices, I am endlessly grateful for your boundless generosity and selflessness.

Mom, your nurturing and patience have been a source of comfort and strength for me. Your wisdom and kindness have taught me invaluable lessons about compassion and resilience.

Dad, your hard work, determination, and integrity have been a constant source of inspiration. Your quiet strength and steady presence have guided me through life's challenges.

Together, you've provided me with a safe and loving home, filled with laughter, warmth, and cherished memories. You've always believed in me, even when I doubted myself, and for that, I am eternally grateful.

As I navigate through life's twists and turns, I often find myself reflecting on the values you've instilled in me. Your unconditional love has given me the courage to pursue my dreams and embrace life's opportunities with open arms.

Please know that your love is the cornerstone of my happiness and success.

I carry it with me wherever I go.

To my grandmother, my Golden Girl, thank you for loving me unconditionally. I will always remember how you just wanted to make sure your little Angel was okay.

In your embrace, I have always found solace and acceptance. Whether near or far your love knows no bounds. I hope I made you proud.

I am forever your little angel.

To my brother Michael, I love you, boo. I will forever be your biggest cheerleader. Thank you for always being there and believing in me. I don't think you know how much you mean to me. Your presence in my life has made it richer, more meaningful, and infinitely more joyful. From childhood adventures to navigating the complexities of adulthood, we've stood by each other's side, faced challenges head-on, and celebrated victories together. Thank you for being the incredible brother that you are.

I am blessed to have you in my life, and I treasure our bond more than words can express. I cherish the memories we've created together and look forward to many more shared experiences in the future. No matter where life takes us, please remember that you'll always have a special place in my heart.

To Shaneka. You're not just my sister-in-law, that's weird. You're my sister in love. I am so grateful for your sweet disposition. You are not just someone I am related to by marriage; you are a cherished friend and member of our family, a blessing that we hold dear in our hearts forever.

To my children Davynn and Jayden, you make me better. You are the reason I get up every morning. You are my heartbeats, and I love you more than I love myself.

Watching you grow has been one of the greatest joys of my life. Your curiosity, determination, and kindness never cease to amaze me. I want you to remember that life is a journey filled with both challenges and triumphs. Look at me, for example. You have seen me face many challenges.

I want you to embrace each moment with an open heart and mind. Always follow your dreams and never be afraid to chase what makes you happy. Passion drives purpose, and purpose leads to fulfillment.

As siblings, you share a bond that is unlike any other. Support each other through thick and thin and always cherish the unique connection you have. Life may take you on different paths, but your bond will keep you united.

Remember, I am always here for you, no matter what. My love for you is unconditional and everlasting. You are my greatest achievements and the lights of my life.

I love you.

To my husband, Jason. My love. We have been through a lot together. Thank you for always being there for me.

During the darkest time in my life, you never left my side. Thank you for believing in me and helping me find my voice again.

Love, my dear, is more than just a feeling, it is a choice we make every day. And every day, I choose you. I choose to love you with all my heart, to cherish you in good times and bad, and to stand by you through whatever life may bring. Our love has weathered its fair share of storms, but through it all, it has only grown stronger, deeper, and more resilient.

Jason, as we continue this journey through life together, understand that my love for you knows no bounds. You are my everything, my partner in crime, and one of my greatest blessings. I am so grateful for the gift of your love, and I cherish every moment we share together. It is because of you I can share my story.

And lastly, to my best friends, Crystal and Lashonda. You are not just friends; you are friends who became like family. The bond we have is heaven- sent. You taught me the true meaning of friendship.

Sisterhood, they say, is a journey of the heart, and ours has been nothing short of extraordinary.

You have stood by my side through thick and thin, offering unwavering support, understanding, and companionship. Through laughter and tears, triumphs and challenges, you have been a constant presence; a beacon of light guiding me through life's twists and turns, and your strength, empathy, and understanding have been my foundation when everything else seemed to crumble beneath me.

Some journeys we must go on alone and there are some where we take people along with us to help share in our victories or support us in our disappointments. I am eternally grateful that you have been here through them all.

You celebrate my victories as if they were your own and provide comfort and solace during times of sorrow. Our sisterhood is rare and beautiful, and my life is forever changed as a result of it.

I love you.

TABLE OF CONTENTS

PREFACE

I have gone back and forth about whether to write this book. I didn't know if I had anything meaningful to say or anything anyone would want to hear.

At some point it dawned on me that telling my story was a powerful way to connect with others, share my experience, inspire, educate, and even most importantly heal. This process has allowed me to reflect on my journey and express myself authentically. It is my hope that I can make a positive impact on others who may resonate with my story.

J. Michael says, "Remember, there are always two sides to every story. Understanding is a three-edged sword: your side, their side, and the truth in the middle." Here's my side. It's a survival story full of powerful emotions like resentment, abandonment, shame, and inferiority, just to name a few. Let it be known; I want the story of my life to be a reminder that God is real. My very real God saved me. I'm living proof of His influence in this world.

While you read this book, I'm asking you to reflect. Trace God's hand in your life through your journey, even through those times you may have thought He was silent. Remember, "He does not sleep nor slumber." Psalms 121:3–4.

If I can instill any message in you, it would be to never let your humble beginnings decide your future, to never let your emotions get the best of you, and to be relentless as you push yourself higher and higher. You got this!

If you're looking for healthy practices to keep your mind strong, I can give you a little insight into my process. Listening to music was a great way for me to manage my mental health during my journey. And I love to sing. I love gospel, old school R & B, and believe it or not, I used to be a die-hard Bone Thugs and Harmony fan. Whenever I felt stressed, anxious, angry, or depressed, I would go to my playlist and just mellow out. I would let good music reinforce me. You should do the same.

I have associated a song with every chapter in an attempt to share what has kept me strong. Each chapter is tied to music that has inspired me, or with which I connected, or which reminded me everything was going to be okay. I hope you enjoy them as much as I do.

I titled my playlist "My Life Line!". Title yours as needed.

The "My Life Line!" playlist.

INTRODUCTION

I am Leigha (Lay-uh) Curry; wife, mother, sister, aunt, friend, and educator.

I am a native Houstonian, more specifically East Houston, home of the mighty North Shore Mustangs, back-to-back football state champions.

My parents have been married for more than thirty-five years and still live in the house where they raised my brother and me. They're retired now and enjoy spending time with their four grandchildren, Davynn, Jayden, Kylon, and Norie.

I had such a pleasant childhood. I feel like we were our own little version of the Huxtables or the Winslows. Growing up, I saw both of my parents go to work and pray together.

I don't ever think I saw my parents argue. I am not saying they didn't, I am just saying I don't ever recall them doing so. As an adult (and now parent), I see why that is important. I see how happiness in the home supports healthy decisions and sound parenting.

Every day my mom would come home and cook dinner. Every day we would sit at the dinner table and eat together. And we went to church on Sundays, morning *and* evening service.

When I was young, my parents protected me from growing up too fast. I didn't go on my first date until I was eighteen years old, I wasn't allowed to spend the night at a friend's house, or talk on the phone after 9 p.m. I appreciate now how strict my parents were. They gave me the structure I needed. I didn't like it at the time of course but the way they raised me made me the type of parent I am today. They provided me with structure, stability, and taught me moral values.

Today, as an educator, I see so many kids dealing with adult issues because they grew up too fast. I'm lucky my parents created an environment which allowed us to just be kids.

I am a proud graduate of North Shore Senior High School, the University of Houston-Downtown, and Texas Southern University. I possess an undergraduate degree in Interdisciplinary Studies and a Master's in Education Administration. I am a Texas-certified teacher, administrator, and most recently superintendent.

Originally, I had no special interest in the field of education as a profession. I wanted to be a lawyer or political scientist. I was naturally argumentative, and in high school I was on the Speech and Debate Team. I did oratory competitions and Lincoln Douglas Debates. It wasn't until

I had a horrible experience with a teacher that I realized I wanted to grow up to be the teacher I had always needed.

I have been in education now for over twenty years. My field is ever evolving, and I love it.

In 2003, a mutual friend introduced me to a man named Oscar Jason Curry.

We had already been speaking over the phone for a few weeks before we finally agreed to meet face to face at a Barnes and Noble. I told my friends, over the phone, where I was and what he was wearing just in case. Ladies, you know how we do. "Girl, he drivin' a green Monte Carlo, license plate —. He got on brown shorts and a tan shirt. Call me in twenty minutes and I'll let you know if I need an escape plan or if I'm going to stay."

Jason and I were friends for two years before we made it official. It was important to me that it was serious before I introduced him to my daughter, Davynn. I don't like the idea of having a revolving door of men in and out of a child's life. It is not healthy for the child. They need consistency.

In all honesty, I never wanted to get married or have kids. The idea of being married just wasn't for me which is strange because my parents modeled such a strong marriage my entire life. My disinterest in maternity came from the fact that I am a firm believer in generational curses and because I did not know the origin of my life, my story, or family members, I didn't know what I would be passing down to my children. I just wanted to be free in my little two-seater BMW & travel the world! God had other plans.

One Sunday after church, Jason came over to my grandmother's house for our after-service Sunday dinner. Sunday dinner was the jurisdiction of my grandmother Doris Scott, who we affectionately call "Baby". For me, these dinners were like the movie *Soul Food*. Imagine yourself at the table with all the food and the matriarch of the family presiding over a massive meal.

That's what Jason walked into.

He had only been around my family for a little while before my uncle, Bishop G. Emerson Scott, pulled me to the side and said, "That's your husband."

God showed him who my husband was going to be. This was a prophecy. It was sweet of him, but I did not agree.

Then Baby turned to me and said, "Speak those things as though they were." *Well, heck, you guys are the only ones speaking, I thought.* I wasn't speaking anything because I was okay just being friends.

On March 11, 2007, Jason and I were married at Trinity Fellowship Church, under the leadership of Bishop G. Emerson Scott, the very same uncle who prophesied our union. With friends and family present, we vowed and pledged our love to one another.

We've been married seventeen years now.

Jason is such a different man. He is what I would call a man who is in touch with his emotional side. He was my friend even when I was trying to figure things out with a previous relationship (my daughter's father). How many men are okay with being the other guy; or the guy who is waiting on the girl to figure it out? He pursued me and I denied him over and over again. I was back and forth between my daughter's dad and Jason for over eight months before I realized Jason was truly the one for me. He accepted me for me. Jason showed me what true love really is.

Sometimes we miss opportunities that are right in front of us because we are being picky or superficial, but I wasn't going to make that mistake here. Jason was single, without children of his own, and loved the Lord. That was a win.

When I shared my life story with Jason, he was warm and concerned. He didn't make me feel awkward about it, he didn't share it with anyone like my daughter's father, he didn't try to use it to hurt me. Jason was my safe space. Whether I wanted to believe it or not, my childhood had caused a massive amount of trauma. I had never realized it before, maybe because I didn't want to, but Jason was just so great towards me about it. He wouldn't dwell on it. He would always tell me that I'm such a gift.

Jason was always extremely patient with me as I determined whether or not I really wanted to be in a relationship. I had already been so hurt by my daughter's dad, so I was happy to be alone. I was okay just being by myself, but I also understood God honors marriage. The Bible presents marriage as a covenant established by God. In Genesis, God created the first human couple, Adam and Eve, and brought them together to become "one flesh" (Genesis 2:24). This verse is often seen as the foundational concept for the unity and commitment of marriage. This is important to me. I want my life to be blessed. In Ecclesiastes 4:9-12, the value of partnership is highlighted: "Two are better than one, because they have a good return for their labor." This concept supports the idea of spouses being companions and helpers to one another. He is my helper. He makes me better.

I guess I have no choice but to admit my family was right. They actually spoke our reality into existence.

I never thought the man I had met over the phone that day would be my husband, but what an incredible husband and father he is.

I have two amazing children. Well, when I say two *children* . . . one is almost an adult– kind of grownish–and the other is a teenager. And yes, the struggle is real.

My eldest child is my daughter Davynn, I had her before I met Jason. She will be graduating from *The* Prairie View A&M University . . . *you know* . . . in December of 2024. (You really only know if you know).

I remember when I first found out I was pregnant with Davynn, I was afraid because I wasn't married. I was always taught sex before marriage was a huge no-no. I was told it was a sin. I was afraid to tell my parents when I found out I was pregnant because I knew I was letting them down. Even though I was 21, I was still living in my parents' house, so I was still dependent on them. I had no idea how I was going to tell my mom, and abortion wasn't an option.

When I told my mom I was pregnant with Davynn the first thing she said was that I was not going to be able to go to church. I had seriously embarrassed her. She didn't talk to me for a long time after, but it shouldn't have been like that. I was grown, wasn't I? I mean, 21 is grown. I was working and in college. That's grown, isn't it? Well, they certainly didn't think so as I was still living under their roof.

Don't get me wrong, my mom was disappointed with my behavior, not my baby. Davynn and my mom are extremely close, and I wouldn't have it any other way. Davynn and I grew up together, so to speak. She taught me how to be a mom. She taught me what unconditional love is. Davynn was so lovely that it made me want more children. So, once I found the man I wanted to be with forever, I had another.

My youngest child is my son Jayden. Jason is his father. Jayden has two more years before he graduates high school, and I am not okay about that. My babies are growing up so fast! It seems like just the other day I was changing diapers and now they are driving. Is there a support group for this?

Both of my kids are such great kids, they are not anything like I was. I broke all kinds of rules like sneaking out of the house and driving my parents' car without permission. Mom and dad still don't know I did these kinds of things. Until now, I guess. You know what, let me talk to them about it real quick:

Dear Mom and Dad,

Growing up, I broke all kinds of rules without you knowing. I'm so sorry. I was acting out and you raised me better than that and it won't happen again. I promise. I promise to never sneak out of your house again or drive off with your car. Thank you for reading this book and thank you for immediately forgiving me the moment you read this.

My kids on the other hand would never be so wild. Everyone always talks about how wonderful they are. They are smart, gritty, resilient, and respectful. And I couldn't be more proud.

I always tell people that I am "that mom" no one will ever have to worry about if Davynn and Jayden's mom is going to show up for them. When they hurt, I hurt, I love them more than myself. I am very open and honest with them. I want them to be very comfortable sharing information with me. I want them to know I am not going to judge them. We go through things, but it's how we handle it that matters. I want them to know I am here.

Now that we've met, allow me to share a bit of my wild truth. Despite my textbook childhood, it was always obvious that my parents are not my parents.

This is my story.

Names have been changed to ensure privacy and avoid any unintended associations, but the world will know *my* name, Leigha Janelle Curry.

Leigha means "the spirit of victory." Through my story you will see how I was called to be victorious.

CHAPTER 1
ABANDONED

"God Blocked It" by Kurt Carr

February 14, 1982 was a cold, rainy day in Houston, Texas. Temperatures were in the 40s. On days like this, most kids stood no chance of going outside to play. Nevertheless, cousins Patrick and Wanda Hillsman begged Wanda's mother for permission to ride their bikes outside.

Wanda's mother, Ouida Hillsman, snapped at them, "I said no, now don't ask me again." Yet they persisted.

The children pleaded over and over again as children do. Finally, against her better judgment, Ouida gave in. They dashed to put their coats on and off they went on their bikes.

The thing about having a bike as a kid is, not only do you get to explore some much-needed freedom, you get to experience speed. Patrick and Wanda were on their bikes now, and they were ready to fly.

Wanda lived on Jeff Street in Acres Home, a nine-square mile neighborhood in northwest Houston. One of Patrick and Wanda's favorite places to play was on the campus of McWilliams High School. It was otherwise about a ten-minute walk from their house on Jeff Street, but this time Patrick and Wanda were on their bikes. Zipping through the streets, the children made it to the school in less than five.

Riding their bikes to the school was a regular occurrence for Patrick and Wanda. In '82, there was no social media so outside was still the best adventure.

Wanda and Patrick arrived at the school and rode up and down the campus. The driveway, the sidewalk, the playground; everywhere was theirs to cruise. This was the epitome of natural freedom and innocent fun.

Then Wanda heard something strange. She stopped to listen to the small, high-pitched sound and realized she was hearing *a baby crying*. Shocked by the possibility, she turned to her cousin.

"Pat, is that a baby crying? Do you hear that?" she asked him, in disbelief. Naturally, Patrick didn't hear the crying or even Wanda for that matter. He was lost, blissfully, in his freedom.

Wanda followed the sound alone, focusing on its direction. It was coming from *behind* the school. The area behind the school was fenced-in, so Wanda had to leave her bike to crawl through a hole in the chain links.

She dropped her bike, slipped through the fence, and ran behind the school. As she approached, the sound grew louder and louder. What she found that day would change several lives forever, including mine.

Wanda couldn't believe her eyes. She screamed for Patrick. Her heart was racing, and her hands were shaking. Patrick immediately left his bike and crawled through the fence after his cousin. As he turned the corner behind the school, he could see Wanda frozen in horror, staring at the ground, but couldn't tell at what. He thought he heard a baby screaming, but that didn't make any sense.

He ran closer and saw what Wanda was staring at: a little baby girl, wide- eyed, shaking, and now silent. The baby still had after birth and a portion of her umbilical cord attached. The blanket she was wrapped in was covered in blood.

Mortified, Patrick and Wanda ran straight back through the hole in the fence, mounted their bikes, and raced home.

"Momma, Momma, there's a baby at the school! It's a real baby!" Wanda blurted, in fear and heartbreak and desperation.

Ouida did not believe them, which wasn't a surprise. Wanda and Patrick were young kids with healthy imaginations who loved to ride fast and never stopped moving. Ouida was usually right to question their wild claims. After all, there was no way a *baby* was at the school. How could there be? Why would there be?

Though Ouida didn't want it to be true, she knew the reality of this world. Sometimes people abandon their children, and when they do, it's never part of a healthy situation. For a mother to abandon her own newborn baby, there have to be some serious motivations at play. These kids might damn well be telling the truth. "Please tell me these kids are just playing," she thought.

Like I said, the Hillsmans lived in Acres Home. In the 1980s, the Acres Home community was on the decline due to crime and the crack epidemic. Ouida Hillsman was concerned about allowing the children to return to the school that day because an abandoned baby could easily be the result of a drug bust or a drug deal gone bad, among other dangerous situations.

To quiet the children's hollering and settle her own mind, Ouida sent Wanda's older brother Norris back to the school with them to "get the baby and bring it back here." Ouida did not expect the kids to bring a baby back with them that day. Lord knows she prayed it wasn't true.

Wanda and Patrick raced to McWilliams on their bicycles with Norris behind them on foot. Even though they were moving as fast as possible it didn't feel fast enough. Once they returned, they guided Norris through the fence and behind the school.

The baby was still there. Although Norris was Wanda's older brother, he was still a child and seeing the blood-soaked blanket and newborn baby abandoned on the ground was no less traumatic.

I don't believe there is any age at which that scene wouldn't traumatize. The vulnerability of the child, the clear absence of formal medical involvement, the abandonment of a helpless person, and the blood. Blood was everywhere.

Entirely unaware of himself, as if moving on instinct alone, Norris picked the baby up off the ground, held her in his arms, and carried her back to the house with Wanda and Patrick circling the entire way.

When they arrived, Ouida couldn't believe it. *Norris was holding a baby*. It was crying, bloody, and probably starving. Ouida's first instinct was to put sugar and water in a bottle to try and soothe the baby. Then she called the police. In what seemed to be no time at all, the police, fire department, *and the news* arrived on Jeff Street to see the baby found behind McWilliams High School.

According to ABC 13 News, two babies were found that day: a Black baby girl who was found by the Hillsmans and a White baby girl who was later found by the authorities when they returned to the scene.

Though the White baby was found, she later died without ever being named. The Black baby survived and was taken to Jefferson Davis Hospital where she was treated.

According to court documents, the black baby girl the Hillsmans found was first named "Baby Girl" and then "Black Girl". Later the authorities settled on "Bridgett Williams."

It is unclear why the baby was given the name Williams, but it is a popular name. Perhaps it was taken from the name of the school, McWilliams High School, where she was found. Coincidentally, Bridgett's future adoptive mom's maiden name would be Williams; a reminder of God's plan, I imagine.

That "Baby Girl", that "Bridgett Williams", that was *me*. This is my origin story. This is the story of how I was discovered by Wanda and Patrick Hillsman on the ground on a cold and rainy day in Houston. It was me who Norris Hillsman picked up and walked back to his house. It was me who Ouida Hillsman fed sugar water. The abandoned baby that the news reported had survived and was sent to the hospital for treatment that day was me.

Reporting me found, February 14th, 1982, courtesy of ABC 13 News

My legal name is now Leigha Curry. My name has been Leigha for most of my life. As you will see, I have long been adopted, named, and survived forty years to tell this story.

When I think about Patrick and Wanda finding me, I know it was God's work. Consider the fact that Ouida didn't even want to let them go outside in the first place. Yet she let them, and they found me.

Consider the fact that Ms. Hillsman had every right to fear sending her children back to the scene of an abandoned child in the middle of a dangerous drug torn community and might not have. Yet she did, and they saved me.

Consider the fact that the children didn't just find me but returned to rescue me. And when they returned, I was still there. I was still alive. Despite the cold and the rain.

Any number of details could have gone the other way that day and I would have died. Yet I live.

I have been saved. For that, I will not be silent. For that, I will always worship God.

In the song "God Blocked It," Kurt Carr sings, "The devil had a plan to kill me, I know. But God intercepted his plan, and told the devil, 'No'. God blocked it. He wouldn't let it be so." This is how I feel about my survival that day. The devil had a plan and God blocked it.

<u>Bridgett's Story</u>

Case Worker: Janice Sawyer

On 2-14-82, two children named Wanda and Patrick were riding their bicycle's in the afternoon near Williams Middle School in Houston, Texas on this cold, misty day in February.

They stopped at the back of the school when they heard what sounded like a baby crying. On the back doorstep of Willimas Middle School, they found Bridgett lying wrapped up in a dirty, bloody, white sheet barely a few hours old and she was cole and hungry. They took the baby down to Wanda's house and her mother called an ambulance, who transported Bridgett to Ben Taub Hospital for examination.

Bridgett's parents must have been very young and afraid about caring for such a young baby to have left her at the school. Although, they must have known that someone would find her soon and take good care of her. Bridgett was transported from Ben Taub Hospital to Jefferson Davis Hospital on 2-14-82, after the initial examination. She was found to be hypothermic, possibly hypoglycemic, and was suffering minimally from over-exposure. During her hospital stay, the nurses and doctors grew to love Bridgett and gave her that name. Upon her discharge on 2-19-82, Bridgett was doing much better and was now able to be placed into a foster home.

My story according to the Foster Care Intake Social Study,
Harris County Child Welfare Dept.

9. Verification of Age and Relationship (Verification of relationship applies to both parents and to relatives if the child was living with relatives.)

Method of Verification: ☐ Birth Certificate ☐ Hospital Certificate ☐ Baptismal Certificate

Name of Hospital or Church		File or Cert. No.	Vol. (Bapt. Cert.)	Page No. (Bapt. Cert.)
City		County		State

☒ Evaluative Conclusion (explain):___ Doctor said infant was born 2/14/82 because when it arrived

at the hospital afterbirth was still present on the body.

NOTE: If age and relationship of the child cannot be verified by birth certificate, hospital certificate, or baptismal certificate and are determined by evaluative conclusion, this form must be signed by the Protective Services Supervisor.

Signature – Supervisor Approving Above Eval. Concl.   Date   2-22-82
Visiting Supervisor

10. Family Need

A. BIRTH INFORMATION:

Actual birth or pre-natal information is unknown because of family's unknown identity and lack of contact with HCCW. Bridgett was felt to have been born on 2/14/82 due to the fact that there was still the presence of afterbirth, blood, and a moist umbilical cord upon Bridgett's being transported to and examined at Ben Taub Hospital, before transfer to Jefferson Davis. The estimated birth weight was 6 lbs 10 oz. Bridgett was begun on a Enfamil with Iron formula at Jefferson Davis Hospital and after 2-3 months in foster care was changed to an Enfamil without Iron formula. Diluted rice cereal was just recently added to Bridgett's formula.

*Excerpts from my social study showing estimation of
my birth date based on my condition*

CHAPTER 2
THE PIECES
"Millions" by The Winans

I was in the hospital for a few days, and I had to be treated for hypothermia, but I survived, and that's what's important.

According to the police report, I was also treated for overexposure and was possibly hypoglycemic. I would later be diagnosed with bilateral sensorineural hearing loss. Sensorineural hearing loss means that the tiny hair cells in the inner ear or the auditory nerve (responsible for transmitting sound to the brain) are damaged. In a nutshell, I am deaf in my left ear and have seventy percent function in my right ear.

Interestingly, this would create new and unforeseeable obstacles later in life. For example, Covid was uniquely difficult for me because everyone wearing masks prevented me from reading lips. No one knew of my impairment, so I struggled.

It is important for me to go to the audiologist every year to have my hearing checked. According to the doctor, at some point, I will be completely deaf. Each year it gets worse.

I remember being a student at Purple Sage Elementary School and having my annual vision and hearing test and failing the hearing test every year. I never would have guessed my abandonment (and subsequent hypothermia) was the cause of my hearing loss. It wasn't until I was older that I learned about the connection.

After the hospital I was put in the (temporary) foster home of Mr. and Mrs. Johnny Brown.

Bridgett's first worker was Ms. Sandra Williams.

On 2-19-82, Bridgett became a part of the Johnny Brown foster home, where the family accepted her with lots of love and open arms. Mr. and Ms. Brown were happy to have such a nice, good, and pretty little girl as Bridgett. The rest of the foster family (all foster children); Jake, John, Ken, Christina, and Joe were all glad to have a new little sister.

Bridgett's foster family

Bridgett at 5 days old.

Bridgett at 6 weeks old.

Bridgett with Mr. and Ms. Brown.

Bridgett's 2nd worker was Ms. Janice Sawyer.

Notation of foster placement

I have no memory of my foster parents (The Browns), but in 2023 I did some research and found them. In the interest of their privacy, I will simply say that they are alive and living well in Texas.

Foster care lasted for a few months before I was ultimately adopted by Larry and Antoinette Shepard.

Notation of adoption

Larry and Antoinette are my mom and dad. You'll hear much more about them later.

As I got older, I would begin to realize that the damage done was more than just physical. It was also psychological. Not only had I been physically suffering from the events of that day, but I was also languishing in the complete absence of information. I had been living with this chronic inescapable damage, but I couldn't tell you who inflicted it upon me. My biological limitations became a constant reminder of the secret that was my past.

Only recently have I come in possession of these documents from the Department of Family Services, and they didn't offer many familial details. I was hoping maybe there would be more information. I mean, I did learn that I was found in Acres Home and not on the South Side like I had originally thought.

I was also able to discover the names of the kids that found me. That was critical information for my search. I think I was hoping for something more, maybe a letter, or a witness who might have seen a car fleeing the scene. I don't know, I watch a lot of *Law and Order,* so I was hoping for more evidence, details, clues to cracking the case. All I had were a scattering of little pieces; a few names, a few small details, and a pile of seemingly fruitless documents. How was I ever going to understand what happened, given so little to work with? And tougher still, was I wrong for my desire to know?

Millions didn't make it, but I was one of the ones who did. Why? Why had I been spared? Was there a purpose to my survival? I had so many difficult questions without any answers. Even more difficult still, I began to wonder if our struggles are what give us purpose. What if our struggles give us direction and motivation for growth? This is the idea I find most fascinating; the idea that personal struggles just might be a curse *and* a blessing.

CHAPTER 3
A HOME &
A SECRET

"My Response" by Phil Thompson

As I said, I had no true home and no true family until Larry and Antoinette Shepard took me out of temporary foster care and adopted me. At six months old they took me in. They rescued me. They became my father and mother. They named me Leigha and gave me their last name Shepard (my maiden name). They gave me a home and an identity. They gave me an immediate family and an extended family. Just like that I had everything most people have when it comes to family; aunts and uncles, cousins, grandparents, you name it. Suddenly I was a regular kid in a regular family and knew no different.

Ours was a stable two-parent household in which Christianity and the Church were fundamental. Religion was so fundamental to my parents, in fact, that they started their own church, Word of Life Ministries. My dad was the pastor. It also needs to be said that my mom was raised in a very structured Christian household.

My father (Larry Shepard) and mother (Antoinette Shepard),
leading Word of Life Ministries

This is what they knew. So, this is how they raised me. At this point I want to take a moment to clarify. When I say "mom" I mean my adoptive mother, Antoinette Shepard. She is the only true mother I've ever known. She is one who saved me, raised me, loved me, and claims me. When I am referring to my biological mother, I will call her my biological mother, or bio mom.

When it comes to my biological father, however, I will use his real name. You will understand why later.

Where were we? Ah yes, the Christian household of my childhood. We went to church on Sundays, ate together afterwards, and whenever it was time to say grace, everyone had to say their scripture.

I also had the best holidays and summer vacations. Christmas was my favorite. Christmas with the Shepards was unmatched. There was an abundance of food on the table and gifts under the tree. We would be up all- night opening gifts, singing carols, and enjoying our family Christmas.

When times were good, I would go back and forth in my mind between wondering what my biological family was experiencing in those moments and forgetting about my adoption entirely.

I was very young when I learned I had been adopted. I think I was in elementary school. I remember sitting on my Strawberry Shortcake bed and my parents having a conversation with me. I remember my parents telling me they wanted a baby and that they had to answer questions about them as people; why they wanted to adopt, and things like that. They even had to get statements from their friends to speak to their character.

Years later, I was able to read those statements:

Attach additional sheets if necessary.

1. How long have you known Mr. and Mrs. ___Shepard___? How well do you know them?

I have known MR. AND MRS. Shepard Since Approximately 1975, Although I have Known MR. Shepard Since Approximately 1970. The Lady that I am Now married to Mrs. Verdie Nelson (than Green) was Larry Shepard's NEXT Door Neighbor AND was a good Friend of her brothers.

2. What kind of person is the husband?

MR Larry Shepard Is A mild mannered person, humble AND very passive. He is Not A person that Is Easily provoked to Anger. In Fact, I have Never seen Larry Angry Since I have Known him. Larry has A great Love FOR Children, AND because of A Sincere Desire AND Interest in them would be A Father.

3. What kind of person is the wife?

MRS. A. Shepard is basically the same as her husband. She is A Lady In Every Sense of the word AND Always Displays the type of personality that people Just Naturally Take. Her warm Smile AND pleasing disposition make she AND he the ideal Couple. AND definitely worthy to have Children.

4. Please describe any children in the house?

N/A

How would you describe this couple's marriage?

I would Describe Larry AND Antionette's marriage as beautiful. There is a genuine concern about Each other. As well as For others. They are A very good Example As what A Christian couple. Should be. Submissive one to the Other which Is the Christian that will cause any marriage to be A Success. Hospitality is A very Fine quality that is Found in both of them. You could visit their home once And Feel completely at home.

Continued

Character attestation of family friends Jerome and Verla Nelson pt 1

6. What activities and interests does this family have outside the home?

The Activities AND Interests this Family has outside the home is they Are Involved Almost Entirely IN Church Related Activi And they Are people who Just Like to Enjoy simple things suc As going to see A good Clean movie. AND Attending A good Christian Concert OR hearing A good Sermon From A Fine Pas

7. Please add any additional comments regarding their home life:

They Like to watch Television (Especially Christian programing), AND Entertain people that chose to their home. They Are very warm AND pleasant people. And Really know how to make Guest at their home Feel welcome. They likes to Discuss the Holy Bible with love ones AND ANYone that is willing That Are Guest iN their home.

8. What experience does this couple have with children?

Their Experience with Children is the Nieces that may Love the Children, the time spent with my son (Jerome Nelson Jr.) of whom they Are the Godparent Parents. Mrs. Shepard is Also over the youth Group in Weekly Evangelistic Meetings

If you were responsible for a child's future, would you want this couple to be his adoptive parents? _Yes, I very much so would._

Please explain why you feel they would or would not be good adoptive parents:

I Feel they would be good Adoptive parents because they are two people that Really love people. AND Especially Children. They Are warm AND Tender people ThatIwould make AND Children happy AND loveD iN their home.

Please add any other comments you care to make (use additional sheets if necessary):

I Am very happy to have meet met Merl AND Antoinette Shepard AND I think they are two of the Finest marraige people I know. I Am Also very proud they both work with me iN MY Evangelistic Outreach. "Spirit of Life" Ministries of which I am president.

SIGNED: _Evangelist Jerome Nelson_
ADDRESS: _48814 Gratuith St._

Character attestation of family friends Jerome and Verla Nelson pt 2

These statements, and the others like it, are testament to the true character of my parents.

I'm certain my parents told me more than that, those are just the details that stick out in my mind. It's funny what we remember, and what we don't. Especially as children.

I wasn't sure exactly how I was supposed to feel about being adopted until someone made me feel ashamed about it.

I grew up spending a lot of time with my cousins (let's call them) "Nancy" and "Susan"; me being the youngest by a few years. I didn't have sisters, so they were like my sisters. Nancy was the oldest, then Susan, and me. Our moms are sisters, so we spent a lot of weekends together. We took trips, spent the night at each other's house, dressed alike, the whole thing. I remember them spending the night at my house and we would sneak into the kitchen after bedtime to eat sweet pickles and olives.

The problem was, I was darker than my cousins and skinnier. My appearance made me the odd one, so they called me names, and did all kinds of stuff to me. Once, they created this concoction of bleach, dishwashing liquid, and comet, and told me, "Leigha, taste it, we all drank some, it's good." I must have been about 7 or 8 years old, and very gullible, because I drank it. As soon as I drank it, they said, "You gon die!" I panicked, cried, and we all ran to tell their mom (my aunt "Norma") what had happened. Norma made me drink a ton of milk. Nancy and Susan, however, didn't need to drink milk which let me know they hadn't drunk any of the chemical cocktail. They had lied to me, put my life in danger, and laughed about it. It was so betraying.

When they would get mad at me, they would say, "You're not my real cousin anyway," and outright tell others I wasn't their real cousin. They were (are) part of the only family I knew, so every insult cut deep. They would call me names because I was much darker than them. They would call me Darth Vader, Blackie, or a black roach. This was my first experience with colorism.

Although I may never completely recover from the damage of their words, I have long forgiven my cousins for speaking them. They were kids who had no idea of the power they wielded or the damage they were doing.

Knowing a secret like that, and keeping it, is hard for a young person. Children have very little power over their environment (compared to their parents, teachers, etc.), so any chance they can get to experience it can be tempting. It was probably just too much power for them to wield judiciously at an early developmental level. I think it's a universal experience. We've all said things as children which we regret. I know I have. I am not saying I am innocent or that I never did those things too.

Curiously, few things stay with a person like the words that are spoken to them as a child. And words can hurt. Their combination of severity and longevity make them unbelievably potent. This is pain you carry with you forever, especially when the tangible reminders are inescapable.

My dad is a tall, fair-skinned, straight-haired gentleman and my mom is a caramel-brown petite lady. I, on the other hand, have a dark chocolate complexion with hair very different from my father. I'm not saying Larry and Antoinette Shepard couldn't have a dark chocolate baby with coarse hair, but the odds are very slim. Because of the differences in our appearance, I grew up feeling self-conscious, especially about being darker than my family, so my adoption became my secret.

I didn't tell *anyone.*

Despite my insecurities, my mom always told me I was beautiful. She saw my negative self-image and frustration with my appearance and countered it with positivity.

I quietly wondered *who* I looked like, exactly. I was always the darkest one in the room and beginning as early as elementary school I was the tallest kid in class. I was just *awkward.* I have big eyes. Whose eyes do I have? Whose nose? And lord, let's not forget the small teeth. I mean, they are my adult teeth, but they are so small. Like little Tic Tacs.

My adoptive parents don't share any of these features. This all added up to me not feeling like I fit in. "You don't look like your mom. You must look like your dad," people would say. These are the types of comments I would hear all the time. As a child, the only tool I had to cope in real-time was to deflect. But it ate away at me.

And what about that which goes unseen? What about what's inside me; the emotions and attitudes and personality I inherited? I can be an absolute firecracker, where did that come from?

My natural personality traits can be very interesting. I have little patience for those I can't trust. I'm sure we're all familiar with the quote by Maya Angelou where she said, "Once a person shows you who they are, believe them the first time." Well, that's not a lesson I needed to learn. I have that instinct in me naturally.

I'm the type that can cut you off real quick if you're no good. Once a person reveals they have bad intentions, I am done with them. It's a wrap. Finished. Good day.

Is this nature or nurture? Is this in my blood or a product of my experience as an adoptee? Am I hypervigilant and less trusting from always feeling like I didn't quite fit, or am I just decisive? What if it's both?

Getting rid of bad people isn't difficult for me. What's difficult for me is forgiving the good ones. My struggle is with forgiveness. No doubt this is a product of my story.

I have had to work very hard to get to a place of forgiveness. Maybe this struggle reveals the nature of my impatience? This journey has certainly challenged me to forgive and have the patience of Job.

Nevertheless, I made an affirmative decision that forgiveness is my response.

CHAPTER 4
DOING THE RESEARCH

"Lose to Win" by Fantasia

To be honest, every so often, I forget I was adopted. I would stop thinking about it. My family embraced me, and supported me, and never made me feel like an outsider. I bet (when I was a child) if I had asked my mom, she would have claimed to have birthed me. That's how much my parents identified as my true family, and for me it was the same, but the questions about my biological family always loomed in the back of my mind.

Deep down I always felt like I would go on a journey for this information, but I was at all times conflicted. I love my family and have zero interest in replacing them. I don't identify with my biological family and have zero interest in causing my adoptive parents to question my loyalty. I've already been given such a salvation after abandonment that pursuing answers seemed ungrateful. It felt like looking a gift horse in the mouth. But I was tortured by the secrecy of it all. Surely my honest journey to find my biological family would be inherently acceptable, or at least not inherently unacceptable.

To couch it in practicality, I tried to reassure myself that the journey to find my biological parents was solely for health reasons. You know how every time you go to the doctor, they ask you about your medical history? Well, I used to summarily deny any negative family medical history, even though I had no idea what my biological family's medical history was.

As I got older, I began to pay greater attention to my health and longevity. I began to realize that if I lied to the doctor, it might kill me. So, I started saying, "I don't know my family's medical history, I was adopted."

That was the first time I would discuss it in any serious way as an adult; at the doctor.

Saying the word "adopted" just made me feel less than, inferior, and embarrassed. I grew up in a loving home full of healthy functional people. Admitting (out loud) that I was adopted forced me to experience the feeling of being unwanted. Just hearing the word in my own voice reminded me of the brutal reality that my own mother just threw me away like trash. That's a *lot* to deal with.

This is one of the reasons I decided I want affirmative answers, not just assumptions and rumors. I mean, I always wanted to know, but I think because I never had any real details about my birth, I had assumed there was no hope.

I believe I was about thirty-five years old when I was finally emotionally ready to begin this journey. If I'm not mistaken, the year was 2017. That's when I made my first move to find my biological family. And it was a big one.

My first idea was to broaden my search ability. I could do this alone, but why?

Enter *Long Lost Family*.

Long Lost Family is an American documentary television series based on the Dutch series *Spoorloos*. "Spoorloos" roughly translates to "traceless", in English.

The show supplies aid to those looking to be reunited with long-lost biological family members. They are also co-sponsored by Ancestry.com, which provides family history research and DNA testing to help make discoveries possible.

I needed these services. This was how I was going to get answers, or to at least get leads. So, one day, on a whim, I called them. I would say it was all very impulsive, but the impetus for answers had been growing for over three decades.

The application process for *Long Lost Family* was surprisingly simple but slow.

Any time I had to write out the few vague details I had concerning my very existence, it hurt. The *Long Lost Family* application was no different, except this hurtful rendition had to be snail-mailed to strangers in the hope it was interesting enough to garner their resources.

I wasn't even sure I wanted to know *everything*, and I didn't tell anyone at first, except my husband, Jason.

Two weeks after I submitted the written application, Zach Johnson, one of the casting producers for *Long Lost Family* reached out to me to schedule a Zoom meeting regarding my story.

Email from Zach Johnson of Long Lost Family

After meeting with Zach, *Long Lost Family* mailed an "ancestry kit" to me, asking for a brief synopsis of my life story and the story of my journey. They had no idea my journey was only beginning.

At that time, I didn't have many details to share because there weren't many. I was abandoned, no note, no nothing. And that's really all I knew. Just a newborn baby screaming to be rescued behind a high school in Texas. I must have become desensitized to the facts, because during our Zoom call, Zach was completely floored. Despite having very little information to give him, I think his exact words were, "This is something out of a movie."

Zach explained they would be mailing me an Ancestry DNA Kit to begin the search for genetic connections. The only instructions were that once I receive it, I must complete it, turn it in, and hope for the best. He and his team at Long Lost Family also prompted me to contact the Department of Family Services for documentary leads.

I didn't submit the DNA test right away. The journey had suddenly become so real they literally needed a part of my physical person to track my connections with other humans in this world. It was an intense realization. It had all gone from anecdotal, to biological.

After much prayer and conversation with my family and friends, I decided to go for it. I collected the necessary DNA sample, sealed the Ancestry Kit receptacle, and mailed it off. For me, there was no turning back now.

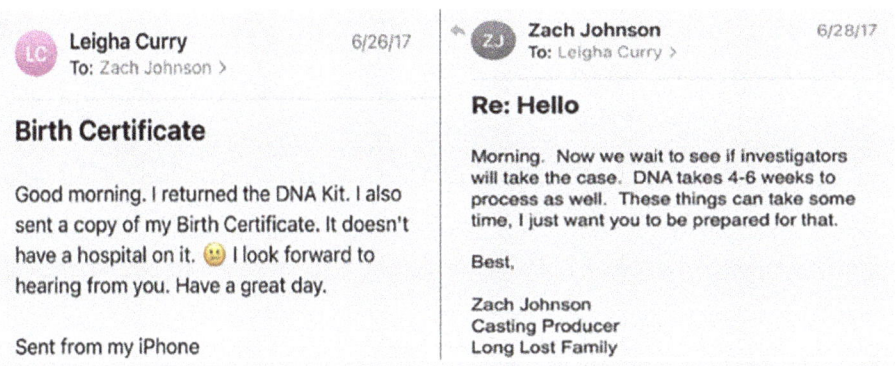

Email correspondence with Zach Johnson

I will never forget the process. I had completed the kit on a Sunday morning before going to church. I remember it like it was yesterday, I was so overwhelmed with emotions. I had every concern. What was going to happen? Would I get answers? What if there are no matches? What if there *are* matches but they refuse to speak with me?

It was then that I realized I had buried the trauma of adoption deep inside myself. It was then that I realized, for most of my life, I had honestly just wanted to forget about it.

Imagine today you were told that you were adopted. Imagine you never knew and just found out. After everything you've been through in your life.

Wouldn't (at least *some* part of) you want to pretend like it never happened? Imagine you were told tragic details about your life that took place outside of your control, outside of your awareness, and which cannot be changed. It's like learning you suffered something horrible in your sleep; you don't have any knowledge of it, you don't remember it, and you don't identify with it, but you're saddled with it forever.

Now, imagine instead you could simply make all of that disappear.

What if you could make the painful story go away forever by just choosing to pretend it never happened? That's how it feels sometimes, and that's what made getting answers even more brutal. It meant that I was admitting to the legitimacy of my painful background.

While Zach's investigators were reviewing the facts, the Department of Family Services sent me a compact disc of all the documents and information the State of Texas had on me as an abandoned child. Everything. All on a simple piece of plastic. It was like a feather in my hand, and an anchor on my heart.

It was Zach who advised me to reach out to the department, and I'm glad he did. I hadn't even thought to contact any government agencies for information. In my mind, there was no information about me. That was the whole point of this journey, to uncover *any* information at all. It was odd to think the government may have always had an extensive file on me just sitting in a folder somewhere; family information about a child who had no family.

I had followed Zach's advice, and now I was standing in my bedroom holding a compact disc that might reveal my entire family tree. It could have countless names on it. It might hold the name of the woman who abandoned me. In my hand. *My biological mother* might be in my hand.

In all honesty, I think I was originally hoping this journey would lead to a simple reunion like the ones we see on *Long Lost Family*, but now that a possible Pandora's Box of truth was in the palm of my hand, I just wasn't sure I could open it. Up to that point, I had been okay with creating my own story. I never had one, so I could always just live in the one I created. But now I was holding the truth.

I stood there silently, imagining it all. Slowly, my every reservation returned as I realized the foreseeable burden of every answer and the possible scale of it all. I wondered what I had been thinking to have put myself in this situation and why I would go down this road.

I know myself. There was no way I wasn't going to view what was on the disc at this point. It was burning a hole through my hand and needed to be placed into the computer drive more than anything else. Like The Tell-Tale Heart thumping louder and louder beneath the floorboards, nothing else existed in that moment but the disc and its inescapable pull on my attention. I had subconsciously calculated a collision of my fear and curiosity and then set the pieces in motion. Here we were just moments before the scene of the crash.

I opened the CD case, placed the disc in the computer drive, closed the drive, and downloaded all the files.

There were *over one hundred* pages of court documents; details of my life that I had no idea about.

This is when I learned my story. I was found on the ground. Children found me. I was on the news. I had caseworkers and medical records and intervention professionals trying to give me a name and a home. I was placed in temporary foster care then saved with a permanent home and family by my mom and dad. I had every detail known by The State of Texas, and the image of my origin story was starting to form in my head.

Remember, I knew I was adopted and abandoned at a school, but after that, the details were fuzzy. For example, I thought I was left at Mading Elementary School in a dumpster, not McWilliams High School on the ground. I'm not sure exactly where I got that from, but that's what stuck with me, Mading and dumpster. I think the idea of the dumpster stuck with me because when the authorities returned to the school that day they found another baby in the dumpster.

When my parents originally shared the full story with me, I wonder if I just twisted the details. I mean I was young, so I am not sure.

I never knew I had been in foster care. How could I have known? I wasn't more than six months old before I was adopted by mom and dad.

Imagine learning these things in your late 30's. We hear all types of stories on the news, but that's the news. I didn't think it could be me. I was the news.

I painstakingly scoured over every document, learning every fascinating nuance of my discovery, triage, and placement. To me, this was undeniably rich with information.

I've taken to telling people I am living in what I call "a *Lifetime* movie," as in a dramatic series like those featured on the Lifetime channel. I joke, but somebody needs to call somebody and make things happen because this is already nothing short of a proper dramatic mini-series, *and we haven't even gotten into it.*

A few weeks later, Zach called to tell me his investigators had decided not to pursue my case. He said my story, and documents, and DNA results didn't produce the necessary leads. He said I could keep the Ancestry account, but I was not a good candidate for the show.

What!?

How could these hundred-some-odd documents produce no leads? But I had learned so much from them!

No one else was associated with these documents? You got a hundred pieces of paper on a baby who hadn't done anything yet, and that wasn't enough to produce a lead? Surely there's something!?

My dreams were shattered.

My only hope now was my own investigative powers using my DNA results. I just knew with modern technology something had to come up. Now that Ancestry had me in their database, it was only a matter of time before some relative *somewhere* was identified. Right?

Well, not so fast. I couldn't escape the fact that Ancestry matches only occur if others submit their DNA as well. Meaning, I had no control anymore. I had done all I could.

So, I just gave up. I was over it. Another letdown. There I was with nothing more than an Ancestry account, documents from the Department of Family Services, and no answers.

I had no more control. I just had to wait patiently for God to choose the right time, if any. This was a situation where I would have to lose to win. I lost my only chance at *Long Lost Family*, but in doing so I would gain the headstrong determination to see it through.

CHAPTER 5
ANSWERS? FINALLY??

"People" by Jonathan McReynolds

Throughout 2017 and most of 2018, I suffered without any hits on Ancestry. Then, in September of 2018, I received a notification. I had a connection! A *close connection*. A first cousin. It was unbelievable. It was finally happening. I was starting to think we were actually getting somewhere. This was a win; a win I needed in my soul.

God is good.

This good news afforded me a moment of calmed stillness for reflection. For over a year there was nothing and it felt so incredibly hopeless.

Most people know their story and their biological connectivity to this world and its people. Most people, even those born into extreme suffering, know the people they come from. But I didn't. Until that moment. Well, maybe.

I had to acknowledge my exploration might be perilous (and my discoveries painful) because there was a serious chance my biological mother did not consent to my conception. I had to recognize this possibility; the possibility that I wasn't the product of a triste, but a crime.

It quickly dawned on me that in my exploration I would likely uncover ugly truths of which it might be difficult to make sense. What's worse, I was also possibly dredging up the brutal past for others; a past they thought they had escaped. But I was tired of being *personally* tortured by other peoples' secrets for over thirty years. I was literally, tangibly, physically suffering, and I wasn't going to be left to suffer in silence anymore.

Being entirely without answers is a particularly torturous experience because it causes the imagination to run wild in the empty space where answers should be. The scariest and most destructive force in this world is one's own imagination because it can explore one's fears endlessly and it knows precisely how to grow them out of control. True evil is the human mind turned against itself, and without knowing where I came from, I felt my own fears and speculations working against me. Miguel de Cervantes once said, "Fear has many eyes, and can see things underground." To his point, I admit to (at times) perceiving things which were otherwise "underground" and visible to no one else. In the absence of information, there was only speculation.

But! With this first genetic match, maybe all the speculation could wash away.

Her name is Eula Nauls, and she became the first in the discovery of family.

Eula Nauls was allegedly my first cousin, though we didn't know on which side. Okay, we have a link! We're doing it! I was going to have to start writing this down:

Leigha Curry (me) – Eula Nauls (first cousin)

A cousin!

This was promising. This meant that for Eula to be my first cousin, that would mean Eula's mom and one of my biological parents had to be siblings!

Bio Dad x Bio Mom   - siblings? -   Eula' Nauls' Mom

```
|              |                          |
?            Me    –    cousins    –    Eula Nauls
```

Now we're cooking. Well, at least that's what I thought.

I sent Eula a message through the Ancestry website and waited. And waited and waited and waited. Days went by. Then weeks. No response from Eula. So, I altered my approach.

Ancestry allows people to manage the accounts of others. Underneath Eula's Name it read, "managed by

Jacquline Jones." So, after waiting and waiting and waiting fruitlessly for Eula's response, I sent an Ancestry.com instant message directed to Ms. Jones.

I didn't know Eula and certainly had no idea how Jaqueline Jones was associated considering she wasn't listed as a genetic match of mine. But I messaged her anyway. And that's the second time I thought my journey had ended.

Years passed without a response. *Years*. I didn't hear from the account whatsoever. I had gone about living my life; busy with my husband, children, and work.

And then, in 2022, a message from Jaqueline. A simple message; "Hello." This was all well and good, but Jacqueline wasn't responding with enough speed or detail for my liking. I was suddenly closer than I had ever been and yet tortured by the casual timing and unknowing indifference of a stranger. I had come for answers, and this connection reinforced the idea that it was real and possible.

I was technically getting some traction, but my engine of discovery needed more power; more speed. This delayed response spurred me forward. It was time to get proactive. It was time to call in the reinforcements.

Do you have that one friend who can track anybody or anything anywhere within minutes? Well, for me that friend is Crystal Bailey. She's my unofficial all-knowing freelance "findoutologist."

Crystal and I have been friends since the third grade. She and Lashonda Hollis are two of my closest friends. They are what I like to call my Vault Friends.

A Vault Friend is a friend who can be trusted completely with confidential information. Metaphorically, Crystal and Lashonda are like two secure walking vaults, holding all my secrets safely and ensuring they are not shared with anyone else. They are trustworthy, loyal, and non-judgmental. They are my sisters.

They have been on this rollercoaster with me from the beginning. I am so grateful for their love and support.

When it comes to Lashonda, I wonder if God told her we would be friends before we ever met. This is an excerpt from a letter Lashonda wrote about our friendship:

> "As a little girl I would have this recurring dream that someone would leave a baby in a blanket on my front porch. In the dream, I'd wake up in the morning, head outside to play, and as I opened the door, I'd find the baby wrapped in a blanket. I'd unwrap the baby to find these big eyes staring at me. Then bring her inside and beg my mamma to keep her. I was an only child and always longed to have a little sister. I had this dream so often, I started to feel like it was God speaking to me in my dreams and that one day this dream would come true. I had such high hopes that whenever I'd experience that dream, I'd rush up in the morning and go check the porch looking for that baby.
>
> One day I sat by my lonesome on the curb in front of the house and as I looked down the street,

I saw a tall man teaching a little cute brown girl to ride her tiny blue and white strawberry shortcake bike. As they made their way down to the culde-sac where I sat, the first thing I noticed about this little girl were her big bright eyes. They somehow looked familiar to me although we'd never met before. Our parents became acquainted, and me and the little girl became friends. It was strange but for a while my recurring dream about the baby in a blanket stopped.

Over the next few years our friendship grew. We became latch-key kids together and were thick as thieves. One day I had another dream about a baby in a blanket, only this time it was different. I dreamt there was a little boy and girl riding their bikes and heard a baby crying behind a church. The duo went to explore and found a little baby in a blanket and took her home. A short time following this dream we were at your house after school, and you began to show me newspaper clippings about a baby being found by two kids. As I read all this it reminded me of the dream I'd recently had. You went on to tell me you were that baby! Words couldn't describe my feelings. But there was something in my heart telling me that you were the baby in my dreams! You were the baby girl I'd begged my momma to keep!! I couldn't explain it then and still can't to this day. But God!"

Can you believe she dreamt of finding an abandoned baby only to become best friends with someone who was abandoned? According to the National Safe Haven Alliance, only a few dozen babies are abandoned each year in America. The chances of Lashonda even meeting someone in my situation are essentially zero. Yet she had a vision of nurturing an abandoned child and we are the closest of friends some thirty years later.

God is good. I digress.

It was time to play detective. Crystal took Jacqueline's picture from Ancestry and did a reverse image search through Google. This led us to Jacqueline's LinkedIn account. I had never needed LinkedIn professionally, so I had to create an account for the first time to be able to send her a message.

The entire process reminded me of an episode of Catfish.

This is a perfect example of the unique experience of not knowing your family and searching for answers. Ninety-nine percent of you signed up for LinkedIn to get a job. That's what it's for. I, on the other hand, signed up for LinkedIn to find my family. Maybe this gives you a glimpse into the nuanced and unpredictable differences an abandoned child might experience. This is just a single example of the infinite unique experiences through which we live.

Anyways, it was September 2nd, 2022 when I sent a LinkedIn message to Jaqueline Jones. Even though this was a strong lead, I was still at the mercy of others. If no one responded, what would it matter that I had begun making connections? It made me realize how dependent we are on other people; in my case, good friends, and willing strangers.

CHAPTER 6
SUNLIGHT THROUGH THE CLOUDS

"Broken People" by Israel Houghton

As I restarted this waiting game I had been perfecting, again, my mind went back and forth. Why *would* Jaqueline respond? She probably thinks I'm just a crazy person trying to harass her or this is some kind of new scam.

Why would Jaqueline *not* respond? Clearly, I'm just a person reaching out trying to find her family. Surely that means something to her. Then again, what if she never uses her LinkedIn account? What if she doesn't sign on for another six months? Or a year?

Round and round and round my thoughts swirled wondering, hoping, praying that this lead would bring me closer to the truth. Why would God give me such a lead only to have it be fruitless. That would be torturous.

And then she responded. Only three days later. On September 5th, 2022, Jaqueline Jones responded!

Those three days felt like an eternity, every second imagining all the ways in which her response might change my life, and it did, only not in any way I had predicted.

She was accepting and inviting! She said she wanted to help me find my biological family. So, Jacqueline and I started emailing each other.

In her emails, she would reference "EN", Eula Nauls. Jaqueline told me she saw where Eula was in my DNA line, but there was no way Eula Nauls could be my first cousin because Eula Nauls is Jaqueline's *87-year-old* mother!

This was too strange. Eula Nauls is Jaqueline Jones' mother? And she's 87 years old? At that time, I was just turning 40, so there was no way I could have an 87-year-old cousin, right? My biological mother would likely be in her 60's, so at that age, Eula was more likely two generations before me and a generation above my mother. Eula and my biological mother were not likely siblings, they were likely aunt and niece, meaning Eula was probably my great aunt.

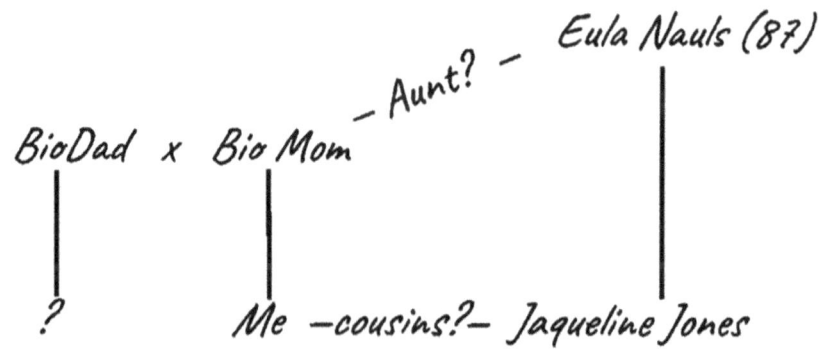

That would be too wild. As you're going to see, the truth is so much wilder than that. I still hadn't determined if Jaqueline was my cousin or not.

Jaqueline and I continued to talk through email where I shared my story. I told her I was abandoned at McWilliams High School, February 14th, 1982, and I was looking for any information I could find about my family. Jaqueline shared Eula's maiden name. It was Henry.

BioDad x Bio Mom —siblings?— Eula Nauls (neé Henry) (87)

| | |

?   Me —cousins?— Jaqueline Jones

Eula lived in Massachusetts and only occasionally visited her family in Houston. Jaqueline would say that she had a conversation with her mom, but her mom knew nothing about an abandoned baby born into her family on Valentine's Day and put up for adoption. They speculated maybe my mother was a student at the high school at the time, but we had no information to corroborate this.

Jaqueline shared with me some last names of her cousins: Rogers, Woods, Bourgeois, Friends, and of course Henry.

As Jaqueline and I were emailing, Ancestry hit me with another connection. Another *close connection*; 1st or 2nd cousin; *Sheryl Henry,* or maybe Lynn Henry, it was unclear. She went by both names. I'm guessing her full name is Sherylynn Henry or Sheryl Lynn Henry or something similar.

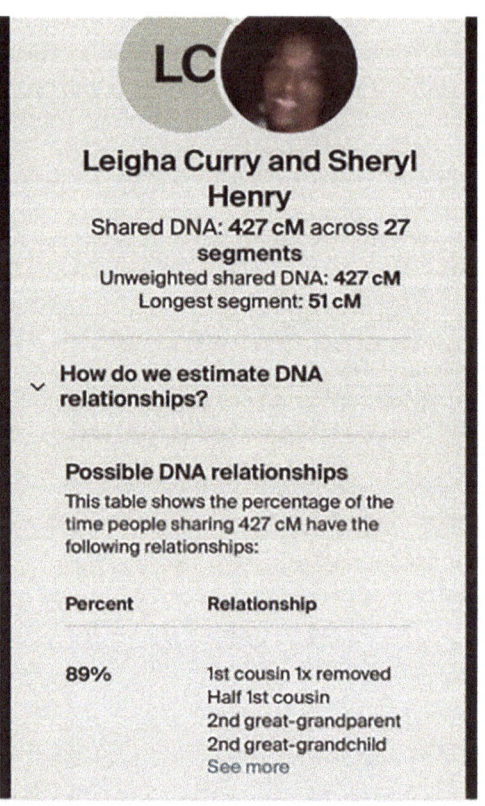

Ancestry notification of familial connection

Sheryl Henry is Jacqueline Jones' first cousin. Their moms are sisters.

Bio Dad x *Bio Mom—siblings? — Eula Nauls (8?) —siblings — Sheryl Henry's Mom*

| | | |

? Me —cousins? — Jacqueline Jones —cousins— Sheryl Henry

Sheryl lives in Houston, the same city I'm in, so I sent Sheryl a message on Ancestry. She never responded. So, I called my detective, Crystal. Crystal found Sheryl on Facebook immediately and sent her a message that read,

"Hello, my friend Leigha is looking for her family and found that you two are related." Still, there was no response.

Through further research, Crystal located Sheryl's granddaughter (who shall remain nameless). She sent the granddaughter a message and gave her my number to give to Sheryl. Sheryl responded in a text message, and it began a short dialogue. I would say we communicated via text and phone conversation a total of maybe three times.

In this story, you will see some people leave as quickly as they arrive. Such is the nature of a journey like mine.

At one point, Sheryl asked for a picture of me, so I shared one with her. Looking back, I feel like my communication with Sheryl may have been too soon. I was so eager to find out as much as I could that I got ahead of myself and lost the secure feeling of a measured approach.

At every point in my search, I was worried that if I was too aggressive it would drive people away. I was worried, ironically, that if I shared too much information, or was too forward, the intensity of the subject matter and the fear of implication would cause others to avoid involvement.

There's a reason I was conceived, birthed, and abandoned in secret. These behaviors, and the reasons a woman might choose them, are incredibly taboo, so for my biological mother to have actually gone through it all suggests a dark truth. Uncovering dark truths that have been intentionally hidden can easily scare others away, especially when it is unclear what effect one's participation might have on others. At all times in my journey, I felt the need to pursue my truth with persistence, but at a measured pace so as not to frighten anyone into silence. If I burned too hot, my leads would dry up. This was my fear with Sheryl.

After I sent her my pictures, I didn't hear from her for about two weeks. When I finally did hear from Sheryl, all I got was a whole lot of deflection. It was weird. I just felt like she knew more than she was letting on.

When Sheryl saw my picture, she said I didn't look like anyone in her family. Even after the DNA proved that we were related she maintained I didn't look like her relatives. Eventually she would claim I looked like her first cousin, but her first cousin is deceased. My exact words to her were, "It's easy to say I look like someone who is deceased."

I know it sounds harsh, but I just felt like she wasn't being completely honest with me. It's easy to compare me to a dead person. That's a truth that I would never have the chance to confirm in person. I could always compare myself to a picture of her, but there was no chance of ever meeting her face to face.

Whenever I spoke with Sheryl, I always felt like I was giving more information than I was receiving. It also didn't help that she wasn't as responsive to me after seeing my picture. This made me feel as though she knew more than what she was sharing with me. I have some very distinct features, big eyes, small teeth, and full lips. I have always wondered if she saw one of her family members when she looked at me. Based on our DNA we are related. It hurts to think our relation might be the cause of her distance.

One thing I will tell you is that going on a journey like this is not for the faint at heart. You must be ready for disappointments because they will come; disappointments, vile attitudes, and people lying about you to cover for their own behavior. Indeed, dishonesty begets dishonesty.

Jacqueline was much more responsive, and while waiting for Sheryl's response, Jaqueline shared with me that she still communicated with another cousin who also lived in Houston. His name is Patrick Bourgeois. She put the three of us in an email thread together. That was September 7th, 2022.

Patrick and Jacqueline are first cousins. Their moms are sisters. This is an important detail so follow me, here. Since Jaqueline and Sheryl were first cousins with sibling mothers, and Sheryl and Patrick were first cousins with sibling mothers, that made my biological mother their first cousin and me their second. Put another way, since all the mothers were siblings, all their children were cousins.

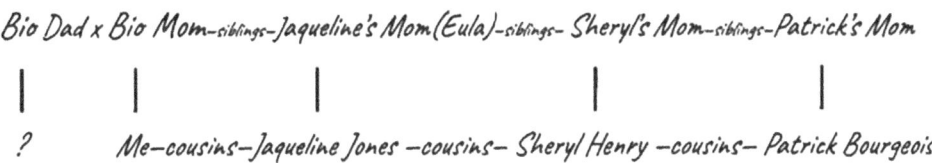

Bio Dad x Bio Mom–siblings–Jaqueline's Mom (Eula)–siblings– Sheryl's Mom–siblings–Patrick's Mom

?   Me–cousins–Jaqueline Jones –cousins– Sheryl Henry –cousins– Patrick Bourgeois

It was at this point I felt like I was beginning to develop a picture of this family. *My* family.

In our email thread, Jacqueline made it clear that Eula could not be my first cousin, she would most likely be my great aunt.

Interestingly, Ancestry doesn't recognize the category of aunt and uncle, it simply lists people as "Close Family-first cousins." Therefore, it was entirely possible one of her first cousins could have actually been my mom or dad.

By this time, Jacqueline and Patrick had yet to see a picture of me. I emailed my picture to them and asked them If I looked like anyone else. That's when I received this powerful response.

Jacqueline said, "You are the child of one of my first cousins, and most likely a female not one of the males. There is a saying, "What is done in the dark, will come to the light. This could not be truer than in your situation. In 1982 there was no ancestry.com, but here we are today, with you now being linked to your biological family. All will be revealed."

September 11th, 2022 was the last email correspondence with Jacqueline and Patrick. Two days later we graduated to a text thread among cousins. Now, he is *cousin* Patrick, and she is *cousin* Jackie, or Jaki for short.

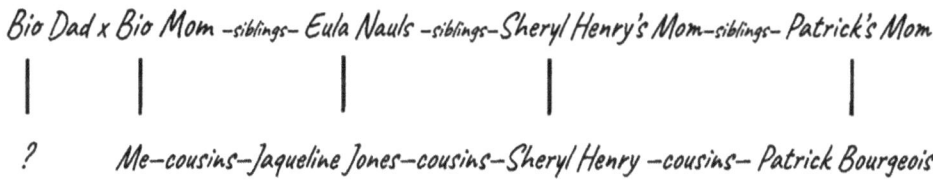

Bio Dad x Bio Mom –siblings– Eula Nauls –siblings– Sheryl Henry's Mom –siblings– Patrick's Mom

? Me–cousins–Jaqueline Jones–cousins–Sheryl Henry –cousins– Patrick Bourgeois

Our text thread started on September 13th, and we didn't waste any time. Technology is something else, you know? I went from not having any hits on Ancestry, to identifying a great aunt and three cousins.

Jaki and Patrick began working tirelessly to help me find answers. Patrick's dad is a native Houstonian and a long-time resident of Acres Homes. Patrick said his dad had long heard about a baby being abandoned at McWilliams. He vaguely remembered the story, but not many details.

Jaki and Patrick were just as shocked to learn that one of their cousins could have potentially had a baby and kept it a secret for over 40 years, so they were invested.

At this point, Ancestry was providing the leads and Facebook had proved itself to be the go-to for follow-ups. But not my Facebook. It's complicated.

You see, I actively avoid Facebook. I have since 2005 or 2006. And yes, I understand this seems like a contradiction, so let me take a minute to address the subject of social media and my avoidance of Facebook, despite my journey.

Social media often feels draining to me. It is depressing. Most of what I see is triggering for me. Stories of people not taking care of their kids? Triggering. Fighting? Triggering. Death? Triggering. I feel like it's just too much of the worst of humanity. I see the intensity of it all and can only lament the fact that it's made worse by being made public.

Why do people have to post *all* of their personal business on social media? I know it's a way to stay in touch and connected, but it feels like at least some things should be left private, out of sheer respect for oneself and others. For example, in my journey, as I made connections and discoveries, I made them privately. So that the other party had control as well. Facebook just feels like the opposite of that.

In short, it's just too overwhelming. On social media, you feel forced to open yourself up to tragedy, disappointment, critiques, and unnecessary drama. We already have so much going on, why add to it? This is why I became reliant on Crystal, Lashonda, Jason, Patrick, and Jaki to find information for me. I was at their mercy for clues and answers.

I was glad I had a support team, because once my picture started circulating and people were getting wind that I was asking questions, things got a little heated. The more I pushed for information, the more it appeared as if many people wanted to keep this story a secret. Rumors made their way back to me that more and more people were learning of my story and there was a significant contingent intent on denying everything. It's hard to track the date and time I heard every rumor, but I received anecdotal information about how the family in general was reacting.

On several occasions, I received word about one person in particular who was having a very strong negative reaction. Apparently, there was a woman in the family who was being entirely dismissive of my story. According to her, I was trying to ruin the family.

I don't begrudge those who refused to help or decided to stonewall me and others. This world is a brutal place. It breaks people. It can make even a good person balk at the opportunity to help a once abandoned child, because motivations can be varied and uncertain. I don't begrudge those who were too afraid to help. We are all broken people in some way, trying our best to simply make it through each day.

CHAPTER 7
LAGNIAPPE, THE BONUS

"Dependable" by Travis Green
featuring Darrell Walls

Now, to my father's side.

Ancestry categorizes your kin as either "Close Family" or "Extended Family". So, when I received a notification that I had two new "Extended Family" connections elsewhere, I couldn't infer much. However, we determined since Cousin Jaki was connected on my mom's side, and these new "Extended Family" weren't connected to her, they were probably in *my father's* DNA line.

Oh my god! My biological father's family was here too! And a surname was provided!

Taylor.

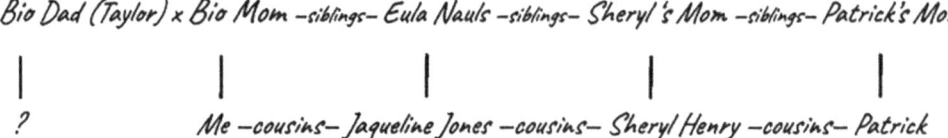

Bio Dad (Taylor) x Bio Mom –siblings– Eula Nauls –siblings– Sheryl's Mom –siblings– Patrick's Mom

?   Me –cousins– Jaqueline Jones –cousins– Sheryl Henry –cousins– Patrick

This was a lot of information to digest in a couple of days. I felt 2022 was the year of discovery. This was the year God wanted all to be revealed. It was time for me to finally get closure.

According to Ancestry, there were two Taylors that I was linked to, Tri'Shunda and Travawyn.

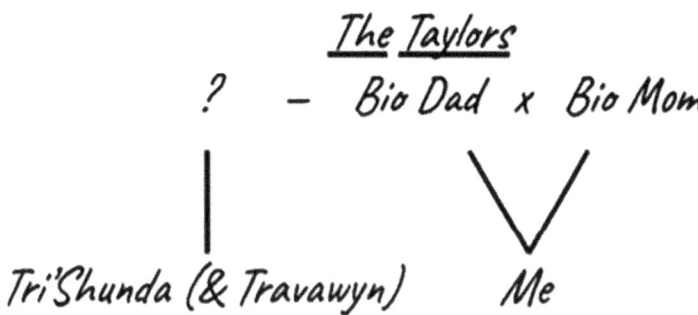

The Taylors

? – Bio Dad x Bio Mom

Tri'Shunda (& Travawyn)   Me

I searched for the Taylors on social media and found Tri'Shunda's Instagram. I sent her a message and began the waiting game all over again. She responded two days later. When she responded, I explained we are biologically linked according to Ancestry.com. That day she told me she was joining my mission to find my family.

Look at God. At this point I had people on both sides of my biological family trying to help me put these pieces together. He is good.

Tri'Shunda told me that she had a great-uncle (her grandmother's brother) who used to live in Houston around the time I was born. I was building their family tree but still had no understanding of exactly how our families connected. His name was either Elbert Peoples or Elbert Taylor. It was unclear at first.

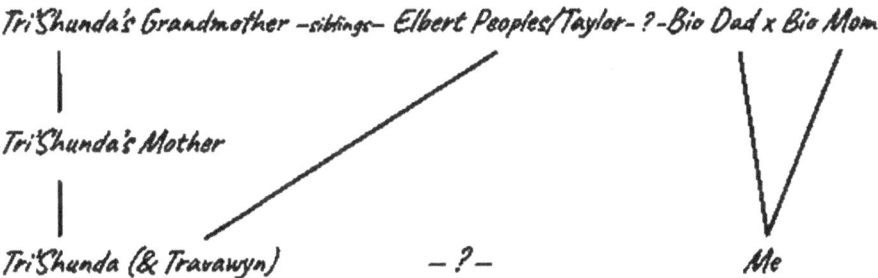

Tri'Shunda's Grandmother —siblings— Elbert Peoples/Taylor— ?—Bio Dad x Bio Mom

Tri'Shunda's Mother

Tri'Shunda (& Travawyn)   — ? —   Me

She also stated, "There is no way any of my family knew about you. If they did, you would have never been put up for adoption." When she said that, immediately I felt *wanted*.

Throughout this entire process, I received negative reactions from my biological mom's side. It was depressing. I dreamt that this was going to be a hallmark story of love and redemption, but it wasn't. It was so disappointing and hurtful. I was innocent in this whole ordeal. I didn't deserve to be mistreated. When I found Tri'Shunda, she immediately, and for the first time in this, made me feel welcomed. She was insistent on helping me find all the missing pieces.

Many people have attempted to shut me out and shut me down during this journey, but not the Taylors. They were a bonus for me. They made me smile, finally. They weren't just new connections; they were my new loving family members. From the moment I made contact. I cannot speak highly enough of their character, for that. I wonder if they will ever know how much this means to me.

Tri'Shunda went on to say her great-uncle, Elbert Taylor (now deceased), lived in Houston for years. She stated that for us to be second cousins, her uncle would have to be my biological father.

My biological father!

Elbert Taylor.

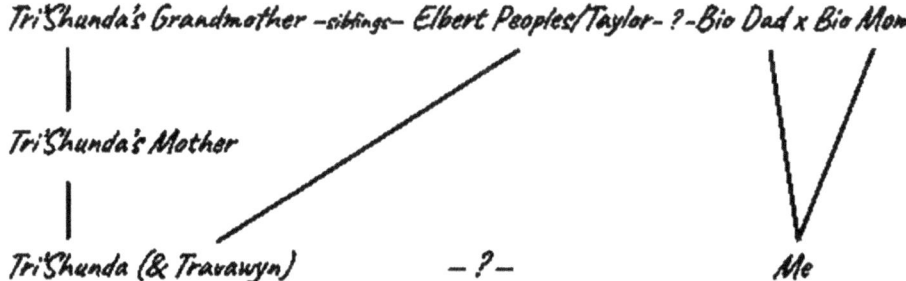

Tri'Shunda's Grandmother –siblings– Elbert Peoples/Taylor– ?–Bio Dad x Bio Mom

Tri'Shunda's Mother

Tri'Shunda (& Travawyn)   – ? –   Me

On Aug 31, Tri'Shunda sent me a photo of her uncle, Elbert Taylor my suspected father. The picture was old and tattered. I couldn't really tell what he looked like. He was dark like me, but tall, which I am not. That is all I could make out. I was so close to being certain, but the grainy photo wasn't helping like I needed it to.

Through Tri'Shunda, I learned Elbert Taylor had other children who were significantly older than me. Those children (that family) lived in Shreveport, Louisiana.

Eventually, I would discover he sired a total of eight children before me: five girls and three boys. I am the ninth.

Tri'Shunda connected me with one of these boys (my half-brother) who would be instrumental in my journey. His name is Riley.

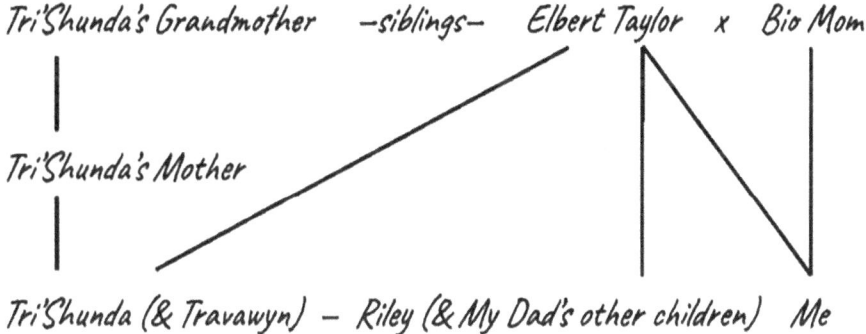

The first time I spoke with Riley on the phone, I told him my story; I told him about the journey I was on. He could not believe it. He went silent as I explained and then said, "Now this got me messed up! You my sister!"

I told him, I wasn't exactly sure.

It was funny at first because he told me I was very proper. He said I sounded very educated and wondered if I was playing a joke on him. He couldn't believe the information I was telling him.

I understood where he was coming from. It must have been very difficult to process, especially considering I didn't have all the answers myself and there were others intent on keeping it that way. I had to explain to him I didn't know exactly who my mom was because there was a growing rumor that my biological mom and one of her sisters seemed intent on taking this to their grave.

During that conversation, Riley told me my other siblings' names; Wanda, Deborah Ann, Flenice, Kristy, Michael, Derek, and Elbert Jr. I was finally learning something of my brothers and sisters! Riley said Derek also lived in Houston, but that the family hadn't heard from him in over four years.

I need to take this moment to say I cannot speak highly enough of my siblings. They have been so incredibly supportive. When I eventually traveled to Shreveport to meet them, I arrived to find they had thrown a sort of "block party" for me with music and food and family already outside to greet me. But I'm getting ahead of myself.

While Riley and I were on the phone, he walked to his cousin Zeno Davenport's house. Riley couldn't believe what I was telling him, so he was going to tell his cousin my story while I was still on the phone. When Riley got to his cousin's house he repeated the story to him. Once he finished retelling my story and how I got his phone number, his cousin hit us with a *bombshell*. Riley's cousin said he was married to a woman named Betty Jean, *one of the sisters of the woman who left me behind the school!*

What!?

Hold on, let's work this out slowly. If Betty Jean is my mom's sister, that makes her Aunt Betty Jean, and therefore Zeno is Uncle (in law) Zeno.

Riley is my brother, so even though we have different moms, if Zeno is my uncle in law, he's Riley's uncle in law too. So, why did Riley call him Cousin Zeno? Zeno can't be Riley's cousin *and* Riley's uncle in law, right? That's right. He isn't. When Riley used the word "cousin", he was being overbroad; he meant it more like "second cousin" or "relation-of-a-relation." Zeno is married to Riley's aunt; therefore, Zeno is actually Riley's (and my) uncle-in-law. Again, for your clarity, that's brother Riley, Uncle Zeno, and Aunt Betty Jean.

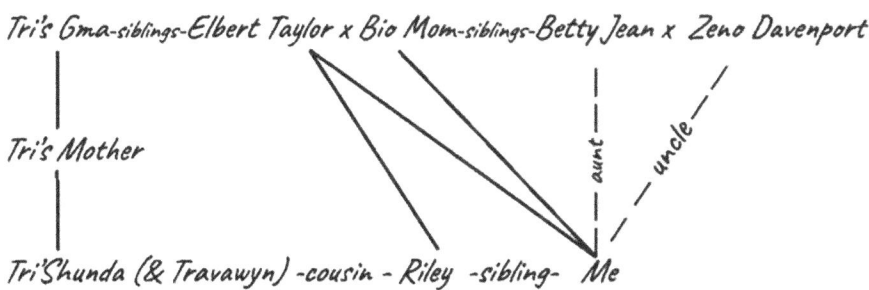

But don't let me bury the lead. More importantly, Uncle Zeno and Aunt Betty Jean claim to know *my biological mother!*

When I asked them how this is possible, Riley told me he had been made aware his dad, Elbert Taylor, had extramarital relationships during that time. Zeno was now corroborating the story from his wife, Betty Jean, who confirmed she believed Elbert had been with one of her sisters, Dee or Jay.

I suspected these were the same two sisters I heard rumors about trying to keep this a secret and make me and my claims go away. I was coming for answers, two sisters in the family were vehemently opposed to my actions, and now my uncle Zeno had just confirmed two of his sisters-in-law knew my father and fit the description. The pieces were starting to fit.

This was taboo stuff, though. Extramarital affair? This would certainly explain why the pregnancy and birth were kept a secret.

In such a short time I had learned of my brother Riley, our siblings, my uncle Zeno, his wife, and my possible mother, Dee or Jay.

It was such an emotional conversation with a lot of information; too much information for one night, maybe. This is when I knew it was time for this story to come out. How could these two instances have so much in common?

I was receiving an overload of information, and I needed a break. I told Riley it was all too much and that I needed time to process everything. I was learning about my potential father, mother, brother, aunt, and uncle all within a single conversation.

This was suddenly moving too fast. I needed to offload this information onto somebody dependable. I needed to get back to Patrick and Jaki. When I hung up with Riley, I sent Patrick and Jaki a text: "New info, let's chat tomorrow."

CHAPTER 8
SISTER-SISTER
"Believe For It" by Ce Ce Winans

In my field of education, we take instructional walks, or "rounds". I will visit a school's campus to walk the various classrooms and observe the students and teachers. I am looking to see what instructional practices and pedagogy they are using. I observe the student's actions as well as the teacher's. On our walks, our goal is to provide the school principal with strategies and tools they can implement to improve instructional practices to in turn improve student outcomes. They are essential tools for the maintenance and development of a school and are taken very seriously.

I remember being at Kashmere Gardens Elementary School for an Instructional Walk the first time Riley called me back. I stepped away and took the call. I thought it was going to be a quick call. It needed to be quick; I was in the middle of an instructional round.

Nope.

The call lasted over thirty minutes. Riley was with Zeno at the time, who then gave more information and shared more of what he knew.

I didn't mention it before, but at some point in this process Riley had asked me to text a picture of myself to Zeno. Riley wanted Zeno to determine if he thought I looked like anyone in the family. It turns out that the moment Zeno saw my photo he knew I looked like his people, which was a strange sensation.

I had gone my entire life not knowing who I look like. I mean, I could have been standing right next to my biological mother at any point, and I wouldn't have even known it. So, to hear from a stranger that he not only knows my biological family but that I look like them was earth shifting.

On this journey for truth, I reached out to everyone who would listen. I asked questions, shared photos, gathered information, and followed leads.

Many avenues were fruitless and therefore add little to no information. I contacted so many people in so many different ways, but my communication with Zeno turned out to be fruitful. Such is the emotional rollercoaster when reaching out into the void in search of yourself. In some places there is nothing, in others everything.

Zeno shared with me that he had a daughter, Alecia, and wanted me to get in touch with her for him. I don't know why he couldn't contact her himself. They're relationship seemed strained and wasn't going to ask, so I reached out to her, using my team.

I asked Crystal to find Alecia on Facebook and send her my phone number. If all is true, she and I are first cousins.

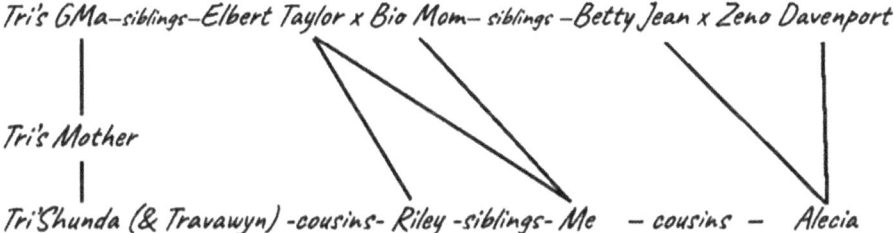

Tri's GMa–siblings–Elbert Taylor x Bio Mom– siblings –Betty Jean x Zeno Davenport

Tri's Mother

Tri'Shunda (& Travawyn) -cousins- Riley -siblings- Me – cousins – Alecia

I met with Alecia over the phone, and she was very helpful.

Like everyone else, Alecia was shocked when I called her. She knew my biological mother had to be one of her aunts, but Alecia said she wasn't very close with any of them. Their relationship was strained.

Family dynamics are funny, you know? It was hard for me to understand how people can have brothers, sisters, and parents they don't speak to. It wasn't a judgment; it was just foreign to me. It's foreign because I grew up in a very close family. My brother Michael and I are very close; we talk all the time. I can't imagine not talking to him. Same with my aunts.

This type of behavior in a familial relationship was new to me. Although maybe it shouldn't have been. My own story is a perfect example of why some families don't speak, and probably part of the reason *this* family didn't speak. Secrets.

Alecia and I eventually began sharing photos back and forth. She agreed that I looked exactly like "someone"; one of her aunts; one of the sisters.

She was so thorough in her research, she even created collages of my face next to the faces of her two suspected aunts for comparison.

Alecia told me that if one of her aunts was my mother, then I also had an older sister who had passed away, and a younger brother who was alive and who happened to live in Houston, Baytown, as a matter of fact. She said she would even try to get in contact with him for me.

Alecia and I eventually agreed to meet each other in Houston one night.

I texted my cousin Patrick Bourgeois, gave him the update, and told him that I had agreed to meet my cousin Alecia. I remember him calling me immediately. "Wait a minute. You are meeting her tonight? Look what time it is. It's late!" Patrick exclaimed hesitantly. I told him that I was not going alone, and my husband Jason would accompany me.

Jason and I met Alecia and her wife at a gas station. I was so anxious to meet her, I was almost desperate.

It was dark, late, and there I was like a thief in the night out for answers. Alecia texted me the make and model of her car, and we waited. She pulled up, stepped out of her car, then I nervously opened my door. I was so nervous that I remember every detail from that night, like when I stepped out of the car, I was wearing a purple dress with purple Jordans. It's funny what our memory holds onto in those moments. I wondered what my biological mother remembers about the day she abandoned me. Or if she even thinks about it at all.

Alecia approached, took one look at me, and was in shock. I could tell by the way she was looking at me that I resemble someone she knew. She blurted, "[Dee] is your mother!" She was certain, but I was going to need confirmation.

We stood there outside that gas station and talked for a few hours. She shared how I looked like her aunts and how I had some of their mannerisms. She told me she was coincidentally planning to go over to Dee's house after our meeting. Well, hell I was ready to go too. At this point, I was ready to knock on someone's door!

I immediately blurted *"Let's go!"* Even though I knew she wouldn't agree to that.

I don't know what I was expecting. I guess I was trying to get to the bottom of everything and got a burst of energy and motivation that night.

Needless to say, I didn't go. If I was going to meet my biological mother, I was going to meet her on my own terms.

Alecia and I agreed we would stay in touch, though. I shared some restaurants for her to try while she was here, and we bid our farewells, and I left.

On the way home, Jason and I sat in silence. We said nothing for most of the ride. At some point, he broke the silence with, "Are you okay?" I didn't know how to answer. I honestly didn't know if I was okay or if I would ever be okay. It was a lot. I was getting so close to my secret past; I could almost reach out and touch it. I never thought I would be at that place in my life. I never thought I would be learning all of this information. The family member I just met left our conversation to meet with the woman for whom I have been searching. I guess I didn't know if I was okay, at that point.

Jason is a barber by trade, but he's also an ordained minister. In the community, he is known as "'Preach, The Barber". When you sit in his chair, you're not just receiving a top-class haircut; his hands and words of wisdom are his ministry. I tell you that so you understand I already knew a sermon was coming. I was going to get the "What Would Jesus Do" speech. Preach was about to ask me what Jesus would do in this situation. I already knew what Jesus would do, and I didn't want to do that. I didn't want to be patient and kind and forgiving and accepting. I wanted to be angry. Whoever this woman was, she continued to deny me, knowing I was alive and seeking her! She pretended I did not exist! She should have had some sympathy and at least acknowledged me! What she was doing wrong! She should have been mature enough to accept her mistake so I could move forward! I was hoping for a Hallmark reunion, but that is not what I got, and for that I was angry. After the way she had treated me, I just wanted to be angry at her and have my husband do the same so we could have a pity party together.

Nope. Not Jason. In his best ministerial voice he said, "Leigha, God is using your story to remind not just you, but others of how blessed we are. We can't be paralyzed by our pains, sins, depression, or hurts. Take all of that and use it as fuel. God created us to get up and walk, not to lie down in disappointment." Then he reminded me of John 5:8, "Then Jesus said to him, 'Get up! Pick up your mat and walk.'" Your "mat" is any symbol used to remind you of where you have been, where you were, and how you had gotten there. You pick it up, take it with you, and keep it near to you at all times. This moment, my life, my story, it's my mat. I take it with me daily. It's a reminder that God sent His son Jesus to save us from our sins, thoughts, hurts, pains, depression, and every other evil and suffering.

I reflected on Jason's words. As we continued in silence, I received a text message from Alecia and picked up my phone. I looked at the notification; it was a picture.

I opened up the text message, and my biggest fear was confirmed. I threw my phone on the floor.

It was her. A picture of Dee. And all I could see was *myself.* I could see myself in the picture of her.

What I thought was the beginning of a long, beautiful relationship with Alecia actually turned out to be the end. Alecia unfortunately unearthed some painful information about her own family through her research of how I came to be. She experienced more pain than she was expecting to uncover (I can relate!) and her attitude towards me changed.

I think she blames me for discovering things she didn't want to discover. She left me a very long voice mail, angry, cursing, and upset. And she stopped talking to me altogether. This hurt my heart. In the beginning Alecia and I were making connections over a love of music and dysfunctional family. I thought we were going to establish more than a blood relationship, but a friendship. We were talking a couple of times a week, making plans to hang out or attend my son's football game, but I think my existence started to bring out her own childhood unresolved trauma.

As I was losing connection with Alecia, it felt like "Here it was again," I was losing a relationship that I was just beginning to establish. A connection to my family. Was I ever going to learn about my roots?

Nevertheless, I am ever grateful for her time, her love, and her assistance.

These are the moments that require my faith in his bigger picture. God will see me through my plan. This is why I believe. I believe for it.

CHAPTER 9
A FLOOD OF EMOTION

Surrounded (Fight My Battles)
by: Bethel Music & Kari Jobe

During the month of September, it seemed like I was learning new details every day. I experienced a flood of emotion as information poured in. It was all so overwhelming. I wasn't just seeing family pictures and hearing stories for the first time; my team was even able to uncover Dee's phone number! This was *crucial* information, but I felt nowhere near ready to reach out to her directly. I had to wrap my head around this glut of information first.

Growing up, I always wondered who I looked like, and now I was starting to see pictures of people who share my features.

After talking to Patrick Bourgeois via text for a few weeks, we decided to meet for the first time over dinner.

Jason did not allow me to venture on this journey on my own. He was with me every step of the way.

That's what a husband does. They support you in good times and bad ones. The vows we took some seventeen years ago hold true today and will hold true tomorrow.

We made reservations and met Patrick for dinner at Juliet's in Houston. During dinner, I learned a lot.

For one, Patrick and I share similar features. We look alike; the skin tone, the nose; we're alike.

You don't have to take my word for it:

Me and my cousin, Patrick Bourgeois

Patrick couldn't stop staring at me during dinner. He said I looked so much like his cousins. We still hadn't been able to confirm with DNA who my biological mom was but based on my picture and seeing me in person, he knew. Further down the road, Patrick, Eula, Jaki, and I would take a photo together:

Patrick Bourgeois, Eula Nauls, me,
and Jacquline Jones (aka Jaki)

Looking back at it, I think I can see what Patrick was talking about. We look so much alike.

Most people didn't know that I was in a deep depression as a result of this. I was not motivated to do anything. I stopped spending time with my family and friends. I was moving through life on autopilot. I am a very social person, often called a social butterfly. I can't say I know a stranger, but during that season, I was hiding behind a mask, and I became strange to the whole world.

The utter devastation of doing all that intense searching only to experience rejection from the people who knew the truth felt like a weight around my neck, dragging me down into the abyss.

I was going to work daily and struggling emotionally. I was broken. It was at this point I started therapy.

I was on medication (Zoloft, Lexapro, Celexa), not eating, sick physically and emotionally, you name it. Jason, Crystal, and Lashonda were the only people who knew my struggle. I hadn't even told my parents or my brother about the searching or the results and we are a very close family. They had no idea.

One day (randomly) I texted Michael and said, "Oh, I have been on antidepressants and seeing a therapist." I guess I wanted him to know. He's my brother and I was raised to communicate and be unafraid to be myself.

Eight minutes later there was a knock on the door. I was in bed, of course, under the covers not wanting to get out. It had to be Michael. I checked the Ring camera, and sure enough . . .

I called his phone and asked, "What are you doing here?" His response was, "Girl, open the door!"

When he came in, I just let it all out. I told him about Ancestry.com and all the details I had learned so far. I explained how people were treating me. They were hiding me and keeping the truth a secret. They were mad that I was alive. They would rather I had died that day behind the school. It's a brutal truth and hard for anyone to hear.

I unburdened all the details of the mistreatment and the lies to my brother. It was an incredible release, and through all those tears, he just prayed with me. He grabbed my hands and started praying.

When I think about how long I suffered in silence, it makes me sad. I *needed* my family, and I had left them out of my journey.

At this point, my parents had no idea what was going on, but there was a good reason. This is something I need to explain to you about being adopted. Adoptees have this guilt that they are potentially letting their families down if they start trying to investigate their history. It feels like betrayal of the people who saved you. My parents have always been very supportive, but I just didn't want to tell them what I was doing. I think I was afraid I was going to hurt their feelings. I didn't want them to feel betrayed.

In my concern about hurting my family's feelings, I was reminded of one of my first conversations with my therapist. He said, "I wish we could have met before you started this journey. I needed to give you some tools to cope with disappointment and rejection."

Yeah, um . . . I need some tools.

I never thought this would bother me so much. I told my therapist that I had a good life. Because I did! I have a wonderful family, friends, and stability.

I had already been found by people who loved me and cared for me...so how did I end up lost again?

Who cares that this lady dumped me behind the school to die?

The thought formed, and the hurt was fresh. I heard myself think it and I didn't like the sound of it at all. This was the wake-up call. At that moment, just thinking about it made me angry. Who wouldn't be? For some reason, the black people I know–excuse me let me be politically correct– African American people don't want to go to therapy. Nor do they want to take medicine. It's taboo. I guess we think our issues will just go away with time.

I see this often in my profession; parents not wanting to admit their child has a problem, not wanting them to be on medication, thinking they are going to grow out of it.

They are not. They need support. They need help. They need the proper tools to do the work we expect of them. We have to give them the tools they need so that they have a chance in this world. It's fundamental.

My people, however, will fight tooth and nail not to have to take medicine, and they sure as hell don't want to admit they have a problem.

Well, darn it, I had a problem. And I needed help. I was a grown, strong, educated woman and I was drowning. I needed help like everyone does. Because we are human, and imperfect. And there's nothing less beautiful about being human. Needing help isn't a problem. Pretending like you don't is. Maybe if we were allowed to admit we needed help, my biological mother wouldn't have done what she did.

But I digress.

I was (am) a wife, mother, sister, and friend. People depend on me. And at that time, I was not myself. I *wanted* to be myself. I *needed* to be myself. But I wasn't.

I knew it was time to start talking to my family about what was happening. I just didn't know how to start the conversation. Growing up, my parents were supportive. No matter what I wanted to do; tee ball, basketball, cheerleading, debate, they allowed me to just explore.

I played basketball in middle school, and I tried out in high school; let's just say I have never been that coordinated. Listen, I almost made the team. I had a fire jump shot. No one else could see it, though.

Still my family had supported me. I needed to tell them what I was going through. I just had to find the right place and time. Then the family scheduled to go on a cruise

Cruises are not my favorite; if you've been on one, you've been on them all. Nevertheless, my uncle loves them, and in October of 2023, he and my mom went on a cruise to celebrate his birthday. She asked me to drive her there and drop her off in Galveston at the port. My dad rode with us.

On the way there, we talked about everything except my quest to find my long-lost family. I couldn't get the words out. As my dad and I headed back to Houston, we stopped at Torchy's Tacos for lunch. While we were there, we just talked.

My dad is one of the smartest most theological people I know. He is like the person you call if you were on Who Wants to be a Millionaire. He is exactly who you want to call. He knows something about everything. While we were eating, I just said, "I think I may have found some of my biological family from an Ancestry Kit."

Eating that fried avocado taco, my dad looked up at me and said, "You know whoever they are, they would be proud of you and should be excited to meet you. You have done so well." I could have cried. I think I did cry a little bit. He went on to talk about how we never knew what they (my biological mom and family) were going through and why they made the decision they made, but to focus on the fact that God kept me alive.

This is how my dad is all the time; always finding the good in people. At this moment, I needed someone to say, "That stupid lady, she needs to go to jail, how could she just leave you out in the cold like that? What if you would have died? She ought to be ashamed of herself. Who helped her?" I mean, I wanted all the condemnation, I wanted someone to be in the angry club with me, but that was not my dad. He ended with, "We need to pray for her. She is probably dealing with a lot."

Really?? What about what I am dealing with? Remember, my family didn't know the depths of what I was experiencing. My mom certainly didn't know. She was on a cruise.

During one of my therapy sessions, my therapist gave me an assignment. "Leigha, I want you to write a letter to your abuser."

I didn't see my biological mom as an abuser, but I guess she is. I asked if I could give the letter to her, and he replied, "Well, that's not exactly how that goes."

Well, then what's the point? I wanted to make sure she and everyone else knew exactly how I felt. I immediately explained, "Um, if I write this letter, I am *going* to mail it to her. I am going to find out where she lives and send it snail mail."

As I'm sure you've already surmised, sending her my letter was not the purpose of the assignment. The purpose of the assignments was for me to process my feelings. Writing has always been a way for me to express myself, so my therapist had me write.

Maybe I didn't want to believe the therapist was correct because of the emotion it brought to the surface. I went through so many iterations of this letter. From sadness to anger, and resentment, and maybe even forgiveness. There were so many emotions. My tears drenched the paper each time I tried to write this letter.

I didn't know how to start this letter. At times I felt like I didn't even know why I was writing it. I think it's because my therapist told me to, but deep down inside I think I needed to. I had so much to say, beginning with "Why did you abandon me behind the school?"

I started there, then balled up the paper and started over. I thought about being surrounded by the family that raised me; surrounded by their presence and their love.

This is what I wrote:

CHAPTER 10
MY MESSAGE TO MY MOTHER

"Deliver Me" by Le'Andria Johnson

Dear Abuser,

Growing up, I always thought the person who abandoned me behind the school had to be 1 of 3 things:young, on drugs, or caught up in a bad situation. My entire life I have wondered which one you were. I have wondered who I looked like. What were the situations involved in this abandonment? Will I ever get the truth? My therapist gave me an assignment, it was to write my abuser a letter. My abuser. It sounds so odd saying it, but I guess when you think about it, you did abuse me. You left me. You left me in the cold, it was raining and you never looked back. I could have died, but I didn't. I am alive and now I want answers."

This was only the first full iteration, however. I didn't like how it sounded. I'm a professional. This letter was going to be professional. So, I rewrote it until it was right:

"To whom it may concern:

I hope this letter finds you well. As I sit down to write, I find myself reflecting on the past, specifically on moments of hurt that linger in my memory. It's not easy to revisit those times, but I believe acknowledging and expressing these feelings is crucial for my own growth and healing. I mean that's what I learned in therapy, so it must be true. There were moments when the weight of hurt seemed unbearable, and I felt lost in the pain. However, time has granted me perspective, allowing me to see the lessons hidden within those struggles. I've come to realize that healing is a gradual process, and understanding the roots of my pain is a step towards liberation.

Despite the hurt and pain you have caused me, I am grateful for the strength it has inadvertently bestowed upon me. Each challenge has become a stepping stone, guiding me towards resilience and self- discovery. While the scars may remain, they serve as a testament to my endurance and capacity for growth.

I share this with you not to dwell on the past, but to convey the importance of acknowledging our pain and transforming it into strength. Life is a journey of learning, and our past, no matter how painful, shapes us into the resilient beings we are today.

Thank you for being part of my journey, whether as a source of support or a lesson learned. May our shared experiences contribute to our mutual growth and understanding.

Wishing you peace and resilience,

Sincerely, Leigha Curry"

This was it. This was the right tone. It was respectful, forgiving, boundary- defining, and from the heart. It was my official letter to my mother.

You know what's interesting? This letter wasn't just about me getting my feelings out, it was also about me letting her, them, or whoever was involved know that I *forgive them*. I can't imagine the pain they must have felt carrying this burden all these years. I know my therapist said I wasn't supposed to give them the letter, so *technically* I didn't, but maybe they will pick-up this book and read it for themselves.

CHAPTER II
SOLIDARITY
"He Won't Fail" by Todd Galberth

Patrick, Jaki, and Crystal never gave-up helping me find the missing pieces. They were incredibly persistent, supportive, and determined. And *brave.*

At one point, Patrick reached out to Jay (one of the two sisters who could be my biological mother) directly on Facebook. He got no response for a few days. Then he called her. No answer. So, we naturally assumed she was dodging him.

One day on his way to Acres Home to visit his dad, he stopped by Jay's house. She wasn't home, but her neighbor was outside in his car. He rolled the window down to engage. He asked, "Hey, have y'all seen Jay?" and the neighbor simply answered, "No. Not today." Not *today?* Huh. Maybe she wasn't dodging. Maybe she was just extremely busy. Too busy to respond to Facebook messages and voicemail.

Through Crystal's continued investigation, I obtained Jay's number, so what did I do? I sent her a text message.

"Hello. My name is Leigha Curry. I think we may be related, can we talk?"

She never replied to my text, so I called her. To my surprise, *she answered the phone.*

I explained to her that I completed an Ancestry kit, and it led me to her. I let her know that I didn't pull a name out of a hat. I followed a literal trail of DNA evidence from me to her.

I also shared that I had seen some pictures of her, and I couldn't believe the resemblance. Jay was in utter shock. She didn't know what to say. She said she couldn't believe that *one of her sisters* could have gone through something like this without her knowing. *One of her sisters?* Oh, lord. Please don't tell me she took my call just to blame it all on one of her sisters.

She claimed when I was born, she was too young to be my mother; eighteen or nineteen years old. Which was a terrible excuse. You and I and everyone else know damn well eighteen or nineteen is not too young to get pregnant. I had enough of the dodges, so I just asked her straight-up, "Are you my mom?"

She said, "No."

I didn't have a choice, but to believe her. Before releasing the call, I asked her if she wanted to see some pictures of me. She said, "Yes, I do." As soon as we hung up, I texted her a few pictures of myself and she didn't respond. I followed-up, "Did you get the pictures?" She responded, "Yes, I did receive the pictures. Thank you for sharing." And that was it.

Patrick reached out to her a few days (maybe a week) after I talked to her. Jay responded to Patrick in a text stating,

"Hey Patrick I pray all is well with you. No complaints here,,,just taking it one day at a time dear. Moving forward... no I am not ready to meet her. I'm simply not an honestly with all do respect, I do not know if I ever will be. Just be 100% transparent. Like I spoke with you before concerning this young lady, she's 100% DEFINITELY NOT MY CHILD. I truly wish this young lady nothing but love, prosperity and a multitude of happiness in her life. May God continue to conner her with his unwavering love. These are my truest and sincerest thoughts concerning this and I simply hope that this will be respected.

Thank you so much. Love you cousin Peace and Blessings."

You know, for such a serious message you would think she would take the time for proper grammar, no?

She made it very clear to him that she did not want to talk to me, did not want to meet me, and she hoped that he would respect that. She wished me all the best but had no intention of talking to me or having any type of relationship with me.

What puzzles me about this is that when I talked to her, she could have told me this herself. But by this point I am thinking I am either her niece or her daughter.

What did I ever do to this woman? How could she not want a relationship with her relative who looks just like her.

Another therapy session was needed.

Why would you not want to have anything to do with me? Based on our DNA, we are related. I mean, look at us! We look so much alike! Looking at Jay was like looking at a picture of what I would look like in twenty years. We are blood. We are family. It's so strange that she would not even want to assist me with trying to find the truth. She just cut me off.

I texted her for weeks. No response. I called. No response. I practically begged her to talk to me. No response. More rejection.

I just wanted to be acknowledged and respected at a fundamental level, but I remembered that my biological mother's pregnancy could have been the product of "forced intimacy." What mother wants to relive that? Maybe I was forcing her to relive her trauma. Maybe she was perpetuating her own trauma by rejecting it.

Throughout my life, my parents kept a book for me. It had pictures of me in it and newspaper clippings. When I was younger, during a moment of depression, I threw it away. It saddens me now, because it was part of my journey. Maybe I just wanted to reject my identity. Maybe I could relate to the woman who abandoned me, in this way.

These deep recurring similarities remind me it is all part of His plan. These similarities remind me He won't fail.

CHAPTER 12
THE CALL

"More Than I Can Bare" by God's Property & Kirk Franklin

As I said before, my team had uncovered Dee's phone number sometime in September of 2022. I had it but I couldn't use it. I was waiting until I was comfortable. So, I just sat on it.

Then one Sunday in October, the impulse hit. Just like that. I was ready. I decided that was going to be the day, so I sent Dee a text.

It was very impulsive of me to send that text. But my emotions frequently washed over me, disinhibiting my self-control in this crazy process. Sending the text to Dee was impulsive, reaching out to the news had been impulsive, and blurting out "let's go" when Alecia said she was about to visit Dee was wildly impulsive. I guess I was desperate, at this point. I felt so close to closure, I just needed answers, and the fear had worn off.

I called Jaki to read the message I was planning to send to Dee. Jaki was still on the phone with me when I hit "send".

I sent it. It was done. Now we wait . . .

I still can't believe I sent that text. I can't believe I opened my life up to the world, but I did it and it was well overdue.

By the time I actually texted Dee directly, many people had learned of my existence and my story. There was a buzz around the family about a young lady saying she could potentially be related to them. I'm sure Dee was shocked to hear someone was claiming to be her daughter, but once she heard the claim, she had to have known it was legitimate. After what she did that day in 1982, and after hearing rumors her estranged daughter was looking for her, she had to be at least anticipating a moment of contact.

Sure enough, it wasn't long before she called me. I remember it like it was yesterday.

I remember seeing her number on my phone as it rang and yelling to Jaki, "J, she is calling me!" I mean, what did I expect from Dee? I had just sent her a text out of the blue basically demanding answers. So, she called. Easy as that, right? Not so much. I hung up on Jaki and answered the incoming call.

When I picked up the phone a rough, raspy, angry voice said, "Well, what do you want?"

That's definitely rude, I must say. As if *I'm* getting on *her* nerves. My momma always taught me to respect my elders, but Child, let me tell you, I would be lying if I said there wasn't a part of me that wanted to let her have it.

I had already heard Dee was trying to do damage control by deflecting when people were asking her if they heard about me. My cousins told me she was also saying things like, "I am not the only one in this family that has secrets."

She might not have been lying there, because I have since learned that giving up babies in this family seems to be normal. *There were more babies.* Three more, in fact. I imagine that's what she was alluding to. Allegedly, there were (at least) three more babies from this family that were either left at the hospital or given up. Why is this such a common occurrence in this family? Why was this normalized?

When I sent the text, I expected Dee might be angry. I needed a response, any response from her. But it was wild to actually hear her not hesitate to speak in such an ugly way; to be so confident in her ugliness. As if this wasn't all her fault.

Although her tone was on the aggressive side, there was pain in her voice. She sounded as tortured as she did angry. I could hear a lifetime of conflicting emotions in a single sentence. For the first time I could hear her humanity and her vulnerability (and even her iron will). This is the voice of the woman who did this, and I can *hear* its effect on her.

At that moment, I felt for her. So, I cut to the chase. "Are you my mom?"

She immediately responded, "No, I am not." Then she rapid-fired questions at me. "Where do you live? What's your name again? How do you say it? Do you have kids?"

Question after question, she asked and asked. I felt like I was being interviewed. "Are you from Houston? You real proper. You sound very educated. What about your parents? Are they together?" She had a ton of questions, and I answered all of them, but I noticed she wasn't quite answering mine.

"Listen, I don't want anything other than the truth," I told her. "Will I find out I'm at high risk for cancer and high cholesterol one day? I just want to know."

She blurted out, "I don't have cancer or high cholesterol!" I was *shocked*. For once I was at a loss for words. It made me defensive and combative.

I said, "Well, you're not my mom, so what difference would it make if you had cancer or high cholesterol?" "Oh yeah." she sighed.

See, one thing about a lie is that if you tell one, you have to keep telling others to support it. So, I stretched the truth again. To call her bluff. I told her I saw a picture of her sister and we look so much alike. She reminded me that her sister didn't have any kids. Ever! I felt like at this point in the conversation the positions had reversed. I was trying to convince her she *isn't* my mother, and she was alluding to the fact that she *is*.

This strange back and forth banter lasted about an hour. Two strong-willed firecrackers battling it out. Like mother, like daughter.

At some point deep in the conversation, her voice became more raspy and she began to sound nervous. She started repeating her words and stuttering.

Finally, she said, "So . . . you just want to know the truth? That's all you want?" "Yes, that's all." I said, in the most sincere pleading tone I could utter.

"I thought I was going to take this to my grave," she said. "I thought I was going to die with this secret. It's me. *I'm your mother.*"

Boom!

Welp, there you have it, folks! I found her! My biological mother is Dee.

After a lifetime of unanswered questions and years of searching, I found my mother.

I need to be honest with you, though. My biological mother's name isn't actually Dee, that's just the name I have used to protect her identity.

You may wonder why I am protecting Dee. She didn't worry about protecting me, why do her feelings matter? The answer is two-fold.

First, we cannot desire a better world only to turn around and repeat the transgressions we have suffered. We must do better than is done to us.

Second, Dee has rights. She has the right to remain anonymous. What happened that day was not only incredibly illegal, but it was also motivated by something profound. If a (supposedly married) woman determines that giving birth in secret and abandoning her baby on the ground is the best course of action, something beyond my understanding must be in play. Something evil presented itself to my biological mother, and the best she could do was to try to make it all go away. For these reasons, I chose to protect her identity and call her Dee.

Nevertheless, after so much investigating, the truth was out! Or was it?

"How am I supposed to believe you?" I said. I literally just asked you if you were my mom three times on this call and you said no each time."

She hissed, "It's me! I am your mother." She was speaking to me like she was mad at me. Like I did something to her. I guess I did. I lived.

By this time, she sounded like she was crying. I know I was. I put the phone on mute and speaker and yelled for Jason to listen in. I knew I would not be able to process what she was saying. I didn't record it, it all just happened so fast.

At some point in the conversation, I had asked her about getting a DNA test. Originally, she was all for taking the test, then she wavered. She said, "I don't want you to spend your money. You know you don't have to spend your money; it's me. I'm your mom." But then all of a sudden, she just completely switched and said, "No, I'm not gonna' take the test. I'm not going to do it. Don't ask me about it anymore."

Her wavering made it so that I wasn't quite sure if it was her or not. She seemed to have all the details and know all the names. She had said she kept me a secret so that *her husband John* wouldn't find out, because she feared how he would react. And it sounded genuine. She sounded afraid. If it wasn't Dee on the phone, then this person was certainly in-the-know and committed to a narrative. I guess it could have been her sister, but that's not right either because allegedly her sister refuses to talk to me at all. So, who do I trust? What is the truth?

The conversation ended and I still wasn't absolutely certain Dee was my mother, but why would she admit to it if she wasn't? She wouldn't assume the responsibility of that behavior if it wasn't her. It had to be her.

This interaction was a heavy weight to shoulders. I had to remember that God loves me, He cares, and He will never put more on me than I can bear. This is where I got the confidence to persist. Because of my faith in Him, I was able to find the answers I sought; I was able to discover my lost family.

Now, I have a family tree. Or two.

FINDING

FOUND
Heritage

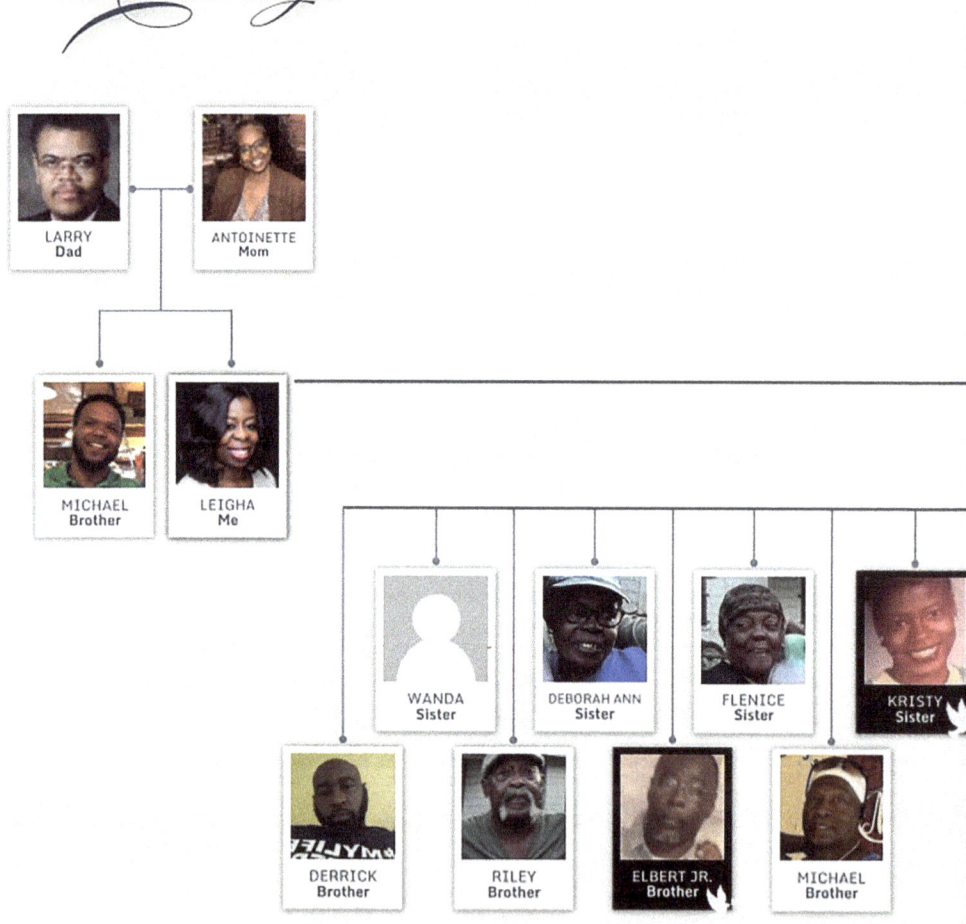

LARRY
Dad

ANTOINETTE
Mom

MICHAEL
Brother

LEIGHA
Me

WANDA
Sister

DEBORAH ANN
Sister

FLENICE
Sister

KRISTY
Sister

DERRICK
Brother

RILEY
Brother

ELBERT JR.
Brother

MICHAEL
Brother

NOTE: The family tree depicted here is not a complete representation, but rather a snapshot of the individuals I have met in the ongoing journey to uncover answers and trace my lineage.This is a living record, ever-growing as new connections and discoveries are made.

LEIGHA

LOST
Heritage

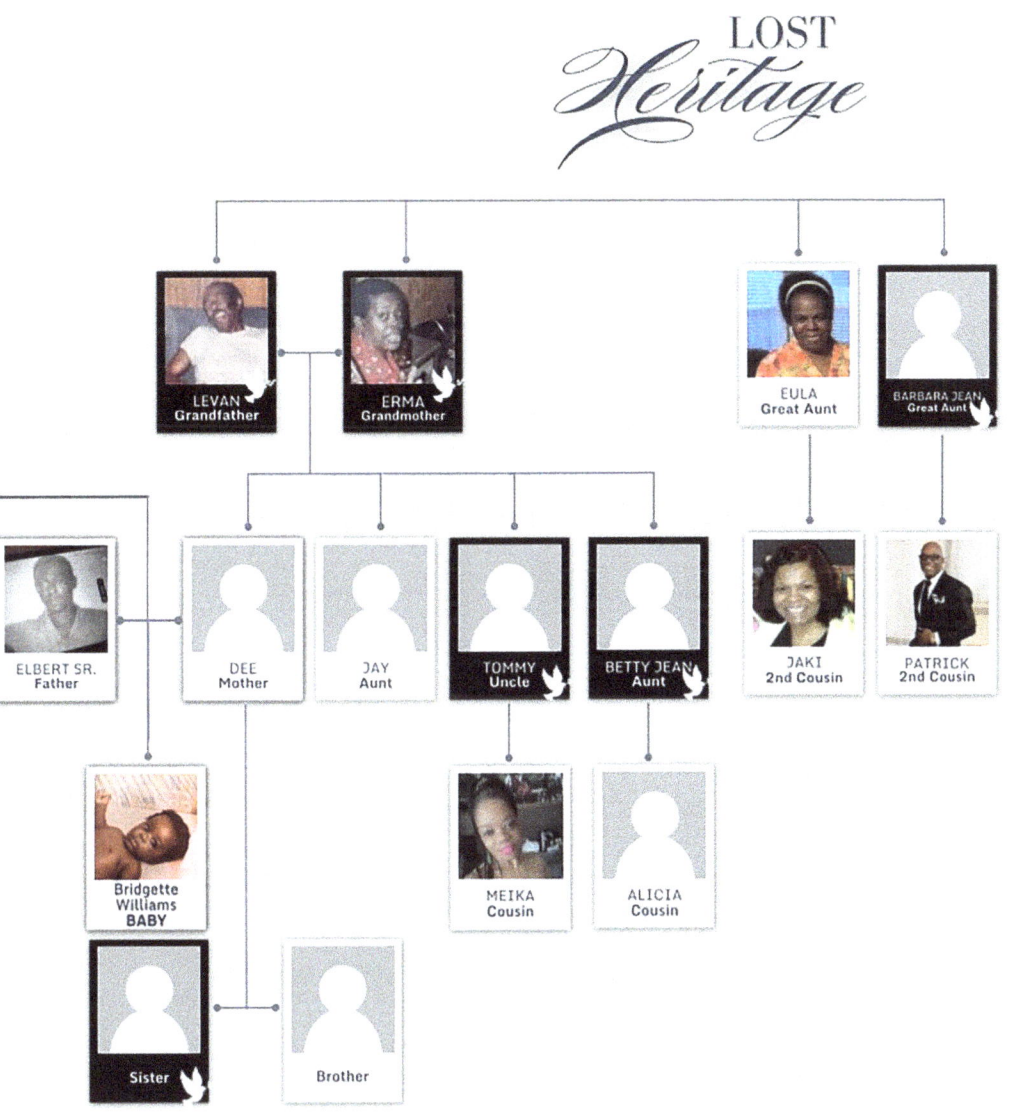

My Found and Lost family trees

CHAPTER 13
BREAKING DOWN

"Broken But I'm Healed" by Byron Cage

Last year (2023), my parents hosted Thanksgiving. The day before we went to see them and the rest of the family for the holiday, I sat my children down and explained everything.

I sat them down, explained my story, then showed them the news broadcast video from 1982. My daughter said she suspected something because she never saw any pictures of my mom pregnant, and her dad (not my husband) had alluded to it with a negative connotation.

This made me very angry. When you trust people with your secrets, they can betray you when they are mad at you. People will use your own secrets to hurt you, and that's what her dad tried to do.

My son was trying to understand and asked, "So poppa is not my poppa, all my cousins are not my real cousins, I'm confused, why would someone leave a baby outside?" We had a lot of talking to do. I shared everything I was comfortable sharing and caught them up as best I could. The next day was going to be a big holiday after a major event in my journey; it was possible the issue might come up, so I wanted to be the one to tell them.

At our Thanksgiving parties, taking turns saying what you are thankful for is the-name-of-the-game. In my mind, I am so thankful I have so much to be thankful for. I'm happy to have this life and to get to experience what it means to have and be thankful for something. I have been given so much to appreciate in this world; life, health, husband, kids, friends, job, and family, just to name a few.

As we sat around in a circle (let's call it "the gratitude circle"), I could anticipate when my turn was coming.

Do you remember when you were a child, and it was your turn to read aloud in school? You would either count all the students before you in line, so you knew when it was turn, or ask the teacher to go to the restroom because you really didn't want to read aloud? You were faced with candid public speaking and you either prepared for it or begged for escape. Well, I was the latter with the gratitude circle. I desperately wanted to escape.

I was holding my nephew and was so glad he started getting fussy. Now I had an excuse to walk away while everyone was pouring their hearts out.

I stayed away for a while thinking they were done. I waited for a while then returned, but I came back to discover everyone hadn't gone and my mom said, "Who didn't go? Leigha. Go ahead."

Crap! I just knew if I started talking and thinking about all the drama, I had going on I would start crying. Not the baby cry. Not the ugly cry. Not here. Not now.

Remember, my family didn't know what was going on. If I broke down, it would have forced me to tell them how I started this Ancestry journey and opened Pandora's box.

Everyone was looking at me. I was looking back at them with now tear- filled eyes, hurt in my heart, and a bubbling gut.

You know, depression makes you feel empty, sick, and worthless. It's like you are there in the physical space, but you can't connect. In psychology it's called "dissociating". You know how you can associate (or connect) with something? Well, this is the opposite. This is *dissociating*. This is disconnecting.

People dissociate for different reasons and at different times. It's something we all do naturally. There's only so much our brain can process at one time and when it's overwhelmed or distracted it begins to shut down less important functions to prioritize the most important for survival.

In my case, I was trying to process so many layers of traumatic information at once that it was too much for me to communicate at my regular level. My brain was shutting down other functions to prioritize processing the massive amount of emotionally exhausting information I had discovered, trying to make sense of it all while also communicating it appropriately to my beloved family and still maintaining control and composure.

My mind was so utterly overwhelmed with thought and emotion, I began to detach and lose connection with my surroundings. At that moment, I couldn't muster an eloquent summation of the life altering journey I had embarked upon. I could only speak very simply.

In a shaky voice, I muttered, *"I am thankful for my family."* My mom looked at me and said, "Is that all? I know you have more to say." And she was right to think that I did have more. I just couldn't say it for some reason. I was too overwhelmed. I couldn't see past all the hurt I was experiencing to the good things in my life. So, my family moved on to my dad's prayers.

After my dad prayed, my mom came up to me and said, "I know you are thankful for more. You didn't even say Lil (my grandmother). Are you okay?" "Yes. I am fine.", I said. Then she wanted to hug and kiss me. That just made it worse. I held in all my pain. I didn't cry. I just stood there feeling hopeless, empty, and desperate to be better. And that wasn't the end of it.

December of 2023 was one of the darkest times of my life.

My family is extremely close. We do everything we can together, and we have many traditions. For example, my parents always host Christmas Eve, and I always host Christmas Day. Every year. We are so the matching-pajamas-even-the-dog family.

For as long as I can remember, spending quality time with family on holidays has been tradition, and the connectivity extends beyond our nuclear family.

When I was younger, we would drive to Port Arthur and spend time at Aunt Robbie's House. The table would be filled with goodies like turkey, dressing, sweet potatoes, gumbo, and desserts galore. I think I had a rum ball one time, and I didn't know I wasn't supposed to have it. Lol.

We would be up all-night opening gifts at Aunt Robbie's. We had so many traditions we would even alternate the order of present opening each year, oldest down to the youngest, then reverse. We wouldn't finish opening gifts until after 2 a.m.

I remember wearing this blue velour outfit and I had red bows in my hair, smiling, happy, not a care in the world.

Me in my blue velour ensemble featuring red bows

We have an incredible family. Those are some of the best memories.

Around the holidays that year, though, I started feeling like the enemy was trying to rear his nasty head. It began to seem like before a holiday, the kids would act crazier, and Jason and I wouldn't be on the same page. Just weird stuff.

Anyways, we are a very close family, but for some reason, I couldn't bring myself to tell them that I was on this quest to find my biological family. I didn't tell my parents until, well, I didn't tell them at all. Jason did. A couple of weeks before Christmas, Jason called them and told them everything; maybe not all the details, but he told them. told my parents everything that was going on so far. They couldn't believe it. Their baby. Why didn't she tell us?

My mom is from Cuney Homes, and she don't play when it comes to her kids. She is a protector and, in this moment, when something was clearly making me suffer, Jason no doubt had her undivided attention. He told them the gist, but the truth. He told them I did an Ancestry look-up, and I found some possible aunts, cousins, and "my mom".

It's so strange saying it. It will never not be strange.

I kept trying to find the right thing to say. I wanted to talk to my adoptive mom about searching for my biological mom, but it was hard for me to just say the thing. I was struggling, and I am not the one who struggles with any conversation. I love to talk. I have always been a conversationalist. It's essential to my success. A significant portion of my day-today is having difficult mission- critical professional conversations, but this subject matter was so personal that I hesitated.

My parents are so supportive, they have always been there for me, so I don't know why I didn't tell them. I think it goes back to adoptees feeling guilty for wanting to know their story. I think it was simply too traumatic to go on and on about. Or maybe I just wanted to share good news only; good news that the people I was discovering were being nice to me and not alleging evil things like I was trying to sabotage their family.

Oh yeah, that was the news that was spreading; that some girl was out there trying to ruin their family.

On Christmas Day, I was still in my rut, still on medication. I went from Celexa to Zoloft and even had to up my prescription. I just wanted to be numb and zoned out and that's what the medication did.

Everyone showed up to my house. We ate, they laughed, and it was time to open gifts. When it was my turn, my brother was acting strangely. I didn't need any extra mess. What was this going to be?

"Leigha, where is your phone?", He said. "In my room." I replied, "Well, go get it!" He insisted. I retrieved my phone and there was a text message, it was a scavenger hunt. Lord knows I didn't want to do a scavenger hunt; I didn't even want to be in the same space with everyone. I just wanted to be alone. Nonetheless I played along. The scavenger hunt led me to different places around the house. The final clue led me to the kitchen where my entire family was waiting.

My sister-in-law Shaneka is always the first to cry. As I approached, Shaneka had to leave the room. That's how I knew this was about to be a crying fest. Lord, I wasn't ready, but maybe I needed it. The final gift I was given that year was a James Avery bracelet full of charms, but that wasn't what absolutely floored me. What floored me and started the waterworks was the letters. Attached to each charm. Letters from the most important people in my life; my parents, Crystal, Lashonda, Jason, and my children. They called Lashonda and Crystal on face time while I read their handwritten letters, and we were all just crying. Crying, crying, crying.

My dad, one of the toughest, strongest men I know, was even getting teary.

Then I realized, "Where is Shaneka?"

She already knew we would be looking for her and she said from the other room, "Uh-uh y'all ain't doing this to me. I'm not messing up my makeup."

This was exactly in character for Shaneka. She is my sister-in-love and her make up is always flawless!

That was the day I cried tears of relief. That day a massive weight was lifted off me. I was silently carrying so much pain. It was time to let it go. The situation reminded me of a saying: "These mountains you're carrying, you were only meant to climb." It was time to heal.

CHAPTER 14
ACQUAINTANCESHIP

"You Know My Name"
by Tasha Cobbs Leonard

My mornings are fairly routine. I talk to the same three people every day: my mom, Crystal, and LaShonda. Every now and then I may have a work call, but my morning conversations are pretty consistent. Crystal and I laugh about how we talk every day about nothing, but these days we had a lot to talk about. While we were on the phone, having our morning chat, I got another call.

"Crystal, oh my god, [Dee] is calling me. Go on mute." I said intensely.

I feel bad in hindsight, but y'all know y'all do that too; bring someone in and tell them to be quiet so they can hear. That was easier for me. I wasn't going to be able to remember everything because I felt I was living a dream. It was too surreal. But then my instincts kicked in.

I hadn't spoken to her since the previous Sunday when she confessed. It was my turn to spitfire questions at her.

"Hello." I said.

"Leigha." The voice on the other end of the call was direct but dark and raspy. Full of pain.

She didn't know how to say my name. I was forty years old and had to hear my mother mispronounce my name because she had only just learned it. My name, my identity, was entirely foreign to her. So I corrected her. "It's 'Lay- uh'; like Princess."

"Oh, Leigha. How are you?

"Um, I don't know. I guess I am okay. I have been having some trouble sleeping," I confessed.

"Yeah me too," she said, "and I have this horrible pain in my jaw. I can barely open my mouth."

Now, this almost took me out. I had been having trouble with my jaw, as well. For about six months I had been having difficulty chewing, earaches, jaw popping, headaches, and stiffness in my jaw. I have tried all kinds of home remedies. I ordered a wisdom tooth ice pack head wrap and temporomandibular joint (TMJ) treatment pills for lockjaw. I even went to a specialist in the Texas Medical Center and after two hours of testing and five hundred dollars, I learned that I have a TMJ disorder. This is the last thing I've needed. Not only am I mentally and emotionally sick, but this whole situation is now causing me physical pain and a financial strain. Who has an extra five hundred dollars just lying around? Not me.

Crystal knew I had been tortured by my jaw pain and symptoms. She knew the issues I had been having with my jaw and how long I had been dealing with it. I couldn't eat because it was so painful. Between the stress and depression, I lost about twenty pounds.

Naturally, when Crystal heard my mom complain about her own jaw, she was freaked out. Crystal immediately texted me the surprised face emoji.

Then she said something I will never forget. She said, "I have all these pills and sometimes I just want to take them all and be done with the suffering, but I have to take care of my husband."

"No, you can't do that," I replied. "You have to be there for your son and your husband." This had to be one of the most ironic sentences I've ever spoken, but I wasn't thinking about it. I had questions.

In relatively quick succession, I asked, "Why didn't you go to the hospital? Did you deliver me on your own? Did someone help you?" I had so many questions and I had waited patiently for most of my life. Now was the time to ask.

She answered very evasively to my disappointment. Even after having confessed her identity, she couldn't just tell me the rest of the story. I immediately recognized this wasn't going to blossom into a complete relationship. Not quickly anyway. We are only acquaintances.

I should be using the word "acquaintanceship" to describe what I have with my biological mother Dee. We know each other, we're related to one another, we've spoken, we're both simultaneously eager and anxious to speak to one another, and each of us matters to the other in a very powerful albeit distant way. We have something entirely unique; something that could only come from an extremely rare context; something only a peculiar situation could produce. We don't exactly know each other so well, but we're meaningfully acquainted. We have an acquaintanceship.

It is unfortunate that I have this limited relationship with my biological mother, but it does not define me. Although you and I might never know one another as well as we wish, we will always share a familial link, and that's God. He knows all of us, indeed he created us all, so if I know him, and you know him, maybe we can become closer and better understand each other. Remember, God said "I knew you before I formed you in your mother's womb. Before you were born I set you apart and appointed you as my prophet to the nations." Jeremiah 1:5. Let this passage be a reminder that every one of us comes from the same place, and before any one of us ever touched this world, we were being fashioned by our Creator in his likeness.

CHAPTER 15
THAT'S HER

"Look Up Child" by Lauren Daigle

At one point in her sleuthing, Crystal discovered one of my cousins, Meika Rogers, on Facebook. Meika responded to Crystal saying she wanted no part of this story and to be left alone. She stated that only seven years ago, she discovered the identity of her own father and that he is a member of this family, and she wants nothing to do with any of us.

At the same time, Patrick Bourgeois, (who was also Meika's cousin) was in communication with Meika. He knew I had reached out to her and lamented to her the reality that few people wanted to be cooperative with me in my journey. He saw me as a family member who should be embraced and explained the same to her. No matter how he approached her though, Meika would not budge; she wanted nothing to do with me. And then she saw me on the news.

You see, I had already reached out to Keith Browning, a producer at ABC 13 News. He was fascinated by my story, so he connected me with one of his investigative journalists, Courtney Carpenter. Ms. Carpenter was tasked with gathering information about me for an in-depth report. I was interviewed several times by Courtney in preparation for her report, and each time I relived my experiences. She asked questions and reviewed my documents, and the deeper she dug, the more details she unearthed; details of which even I had been unaware.

Courtney's report had been ready to air long before I reached out to Meika, and the timing was a godsend.

Then the story ran . . .

ABC 13 News

. . . and Meika saw it. That's when she had a change of heart.

Meika reached out to Crystal and apologized for rejecting me and my claims. She said after hearing the anchor tell my story and then seeing my face, she knew it was real. I guess at this point I should explain that Meika and I look alike. You can see our relation right on our face. Once she saw that I wanted nothing more than to discover my family, and that I looked like her, she was on board. Meika was even so kind as to reach out to me directly, apologize to me, and ask me about the journey.

I can totally understand why a story like mine might cause trepidation. I can totally understand how it might drive others away. As much as I *hoped* everyone would join me willingly, I didn't *expect* it. That's why it speaks to Meika's character that, although she was initially avoidant, she acted reasonably in light of new evidence.

It's hard for people to go against their first instincts, which is why Meika's new solidarity was such powerful reinforcement. In my mind, it was an example of the undeniability of my message. I walked in truth and Meika saw it and joined me. For that I am ever grateful.

Some weeks later, Meika's father (my uncle) passed away. Meika reached out and invited me to the funeral. She told me that she understood if it was too awkward or uncomfortable to be there but that I was absolutely invited because after all her father was my uncle.

I couldn't believe how sweet of a gesture this was, especially in light of Meika's vulnerability and pain having just lost her father. She was treating me like family even in her time of suffering.

I went back and forth about whether I would attend the funeral. I was feeling mixed emotions. Of course I wanted to be there, but I was also starting to feel guiltier for pursuing my biological family right in front of my adoptive family. I didn't want to betray them. I already had so many answers, was I being greedy or narcissistic trying to find every single person and put a face to every name possible?

I went back and forth and back and forth. I consulted my husband, my friends, and God. And I decided to go.

This particular church was new to me and, as I had just come from work, I felt underdressed, so I walked in very self-conscious. I was just hoping to meet some family for the first time when I realized Dee was probably in the room.

It was a small room, but it was full of the bereaved. There may have been forty people there, and in this small space, finding her would be unnervingly straight forward.

The church was old. When the door swung open, you could hear it creaking and everyone would turn to see who had arrived. Once I had made it in, I just sat quietly at the back.

I happened to be friends with one of the musicians, Joshua Alexander, so I approached him to say hi.

"What are you doing here?", he asked. I looked at him with the weight of my story in my eyes as if to brace him for a long exposition, then I began from the top.

We have known each other for years and he never knew my story. I wanted to explain to him what I was doing there, but the context wouldn't allow me to go into too much detail, so in the interest of brevity, I gave him the condensed version. I explained that I had been abandoned, that I was discovering my biological family, that this is my survival story, and that my biological mother could very well be in this church *right now.*

As I was explaining, I realized the woman standing directly behind me was listening in very intently. When she looked away, I caught a glance at her.

It was *her, Dee!* She was standing right behind me! I could have reached out and touched her. After four decades, I was standing next to my mother for the first time.

How do I convey to you how surreal this felt? It was so incredibly odd seeing her actual form in the context of all the myth and mystery and significance around her that I had built up in my mind. She was just flesh. Just a regular ol' lady. She could have been any one of a million regular ol' ladies I have ever seen. I could have walked past her a thousand times without ever noticing her. And yet despite her mundanity, she held such deep subconscious psychological and emotional importance to me.

I whispered to my friend, "that's her!" The look in his eyes said it all; confusion, shock, revelation, excitement, fear, anger, and awe.

I couldn't approach her though. I just wanted to be a fly on the wall at this point. I just wanted to watch. So, I did. I just watched. I didn't approach her; I didn't bother her; I didn't engage. I just watched.

When she walked away, Joshua couldn't believe I was still standing. He told me I was brave for showing up and strong for remaining calm and collected. He was very loving in that moment for being so concerned, complimentary, and acting with reflexive solidarity.

To be honest, as I watched her, his voice sounded like Charlie Brown's mother's. You know, "wah, wah wah, wah wahh." I could hear him, but I couldn't. Once I saw Dee, I developed a sort of momentary tunnel vision and blurred hearing. As much as I intended on giving my friend my attention, I couldn't. Her presence exerted a gravitas on me which was deep and primal. I had to triangulate my friend's words to me from his tone, cadence, and inflection, because nothing could take priority over the laser-focus I experienced being in a room for the first time with Dee.

I watched her from a distance as long as I could then excused myself. I went out to my car to give this sensory overload a rest. As I was sitting out there attempting to process calmly through the tunnel-vision, she walked out of the church. She walked to her car accompanied by someone else, and I observed her the entire time. It was as if God gave me my own opportunity to be alone in my space and view her up close. She wasn't exactly parked near me, but I observed her the entire time.

All of this stress for just this lady? I already have a loving family. Why do I have to identify with this woman and internalize her behavior? Why do I have to be associated with her? I wonder if she's sad. I wonder if she feels the pain of loss for me. If she does, she has buried it deeply because she doesn't appear to live burdened by the emotional pain of abandoning a newborn daughter. What would possess a woman to do something so cruel? What was happening in her life that the best choice was abandonment?

In that moment I saw her as both perpetrator and victim. I saw her as both an irresponsible parent, and a scared child.

The two of them got in her car and drove away. I hadn't seen her before, and I haven't seen her since.

On the brighter side, I was able to locate Wanda and Patrick Hillsman, the two kids who found me on the ground that day. I had always wondered who found me but had no information to go on. I had always wondered if they remembered that day or forgot about me completely. I had always wondered what they looked like and what they were thinking. Thanks to Courtney Carpenter, the reporter at ABC news, I was able to find out. She had obtained Patrick Hillsman's contact information during her research of my story. She had already located Patrick and Wanda and was able to give me Patrick's cell phone number. This was going to be an interesting phone conversation. What do you say, "Excuse me, do you remember finding me on the ground back in '82"? And what if they don't remember? How would I respond, "Oh no I promise it happened, anyway talk to you later"? This phone call was going to be uncharted territory for me.

When I called, a lady answered the phone. I gave her the rundown of my story, but she didn't sound very convinced at first. I don't blame her. Imagine a lady calling for your husband after 9 p.m. saying I think he may have found me behind a school some forty years ago. That would sound strange to anyone. After I told her the details though, she said, "He told me about this. This is my phone; I will have him call you when I get off work." Later that night, I was in my bedroom talking to Jason when my phone rang. It was Patrick! He said, "Is this the baby? I can't believe it. It's really you!" He was just as shocked as I was. He told me that every Valentine's Day they are reminded of that day in '82 and they wonder what ever happened to "the baby".

We talked and talked, and he said Wanda would love to hear from me. I told him to give her my number and he did. Wanda sent me a text message that night.

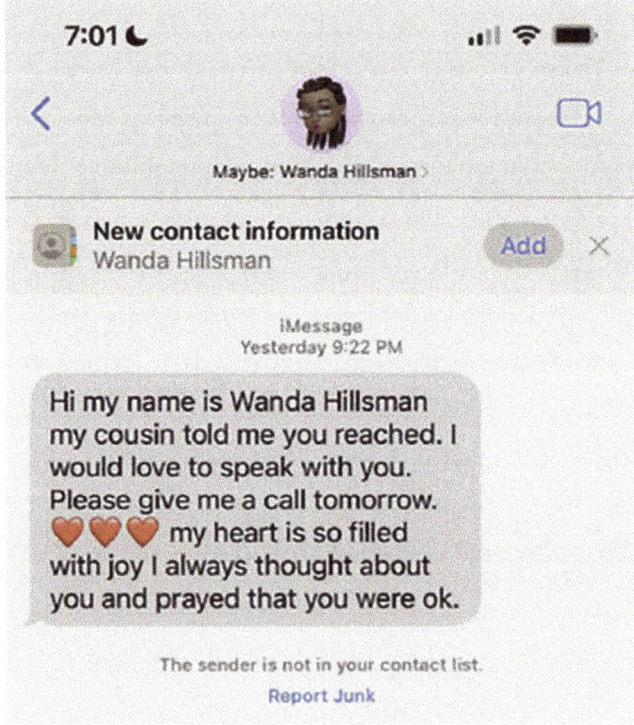

Text from Wanda Hillsman

I was so physically and emotionally exhausted from the day's events, I just read it and fell asleep.

I called her the next day. As soon as she heard it was me, she sounded relieved. Wanda and I talked at length, and this conversation went differently than I ever could have expected. While we were on the phone, she asked me if I knew who my mom was, and I told her I had some ideas. I wasn't sure I wanted to share too many details because I was reconnecting with Wanda for the first time and wanted to remain initially protective of information. I told her my DNA led me to two sisters Dee and Jay, and that I wasn't exactly sure which one it was. When Wanda heard that she gasped and asked to call me right back.

Within five minutes she had called me back, only this time she had a bombshell to drop. Wanda explained to me that, based on the names and connections I was describing, *she* believed Dee and Jay were *her cousins* on her dad's side. Patrick and Wanda Hillsman, the two people who found me that fateful day in 1982, the two people who saved my life, are my first cousins once removed? *What!?* At this point, my story had come full circle. This was just too much. Wanda and Patrick are family.

Wild, right? It gets even wilder than that . . .

Wanda said she remembered being young and having Dee visit their house! She said she remembered strange moments when the family was quietly whispering about why Dee was wearing a heavy coat while it was hot outside. Anyone familiar with Houston, Texas knows there's a very short window of time when a winter coat is necessary, and wearing one any time outside of that window is objectively strange. Heck, a winter coat in the Houston climate could be downright dangerous. Houston is one of those, "it's not the heat it's the humidity" cities. Wearing a heavy coat in Houston is like wearing a heavy coat in a literal sauna. It's no wonder Wanda remembered this from so long ago.

I could not have predicted this turn of events in my wildest dreams. This entire time I had been searching for family not knowing family had found me first.

Wanda Nelson
3m · 🌐

Good Morning Family and Friends I am so grateful to God this morning this week the strangest thing has happened. When I was 11 years old me and my cousin Patrick Hillsman found a baby at MC Willams Middle School. This baby has reached out to me and my cousin 40 years later. I am so grateful to God for saving this Baby. The story will be told soon.❤️🎁From God, God had Purpose for this baby. Wow

👍❤️ You and 1 other

Wanda Nelson (neé Hillsman) posts on Facebook

My Saviors and Me

*Patrick Hillsman, Me, and Wanda Nelson (neé Hillsman),
standing exactly where they found me.*

CHAPTER 16
PAIN, PURPOSE, AND PASTORS

"God Problems" by Chandler Moore and Maverick City Music

I am what you would call a church baby, a preacher's kid; it's all I know. Whenever I have a problem, I have been taught to go to God in prayer. If I call my mom and tell her that I am having an issue, I am not feeling well, or maybe things are not going well at work, she immediately starts praying. She doesn't have to know the details and quite frankly doesn't want the details; she just starts praying on my behalf. The power of a praying mother.

I attend The Fellowship of Purpose (FOP) church, in Houston Texas under the leadership of Pastor Byron and Marcella Murray. Our vision is to create a community of authentic believers and to witness transformation by life changing reality of the gospel, as people come to know Jesus as their Lord and Savior.

Jason and I joined FOP in 2011. When Jason and I arrived, we were looking for Godly examples of married couples, Godly men and women. God led us to The Fellowship of Purpose Church. When it was time for the invitation (the benediction) Jason clenched my hand and we walked down the aisle to place our membership. At that moment, Pastor Murray said, "This couple was sent here by God. There is ministry in them." He didn't know anything about us, where we came from, or our upbringing, God spoke to him and our lives have not been the same since we have been under their leadership.

Being connected is very important. Understanding your purpose is important. Finding a spiritual leader who supports you, prays for you, gives you direction is what you need.

In one of my very few conversations with Dee, I was in the car driving home when she told me the hardest thing she'd ever had to do was bury her daughter. Apparently, she had a daughter (I had a sister?) that passed away and burying her was incredibly painful. I remember yelling at her for saying that burying one daughter was more difficult than abandoning another. How could she leave a baby to die, then turn around and be sad about the death of another baby?

I was crying, screaming, and angry and guess who called me. Pastor Murray.

I could say he called out of nowhere, but I believe at that

moment the Holy Spirit put me on his mind. I was literally ready to drive my car into one of the guardrails on the beltway. I was tired, emotionally drained, and just wanted to leave it all behind. The pain I was feeling was unbearable for me. It was too much. I looked down at the phone, eyes full of tears, I answered. "Hello." Pastor Murray heard the distress in my voice and he said, "Oh my God!" and he immediately just started praying. He didn't ask any questions, he just prayed. Sometimes that's what you need. Someone who can go to God on your behalf. Someone who will pray when you can't, someone who will cover you in your time of despair.

A spiritual father or mother prays for you, with you, covers you, and corrects you if you need it. Jason says, "A spiritual father/mother is someone you trust with your spiritual life. Like your natural father, you trust them to be there when you need them." When he said that, I thought about how we are with our children. Davynn and Jayden, know no matter what, we will always be there for them.

No matter what.

We will always *make a way* to ensure our kids have exactly what they need. We will always protect, provide, and impart wisdom to our kids.

Just remember, you trust your spiritual father/mother for guidance, direction, and instruction. He/she helps develop in the things of the spirit. Being connected is important for your life and your purpose. Who are you connected to? It matters.

I wanted to just be a member at the Fellowship of Purpose. Go to church, hug a few necks, go home, and that's it. But I just couldn't. That is not how I was raised, what I was taught, nor what I saw growing up.

I was taught that we are supposed to work in ministry. I saw both of my parents work in ministry and guess what, I am doing the same with my children. Working in ministry helps cultivate your spiritual growth and develops a sense of belonging and connectivity. So, I joined the Praise Team.

By now, you know I love music. I also love to sing. Even when I joined, it took me a while to actually start leading songs, but once I started, I couldn't stop.

It was around 2017 when I took the reins as the Praise and Worship Leader at FOP. I am not the best singer, but my worship is for real. I am serious about ministry, and now I think you know why. You know my story. He deserves my worship and my praise.

When I started this journey of finding answers about my existence, things started to get very difficult for me. I know what you're thinking, "Pray and it will go away, you go to church don't you? Why would your God allow this to happen to you? Why didn't God restore you?"

Just because I go to church and serve an omnipresent God doesn't mean I won't go through tribulations. The same goes for you. He never said things would be perfect or that we wouldn't go through things. He said it's how you will respond when you are going through it that matters. Who will you run to in times of crisis? Do you run to substances, alcohol, drugs, sex? Or will you solely run to him.

Phil Thompson's song, "My Response" is one of my favorites. Especially the line, "You have rescued my life, I'm never going back." I encourage you to make a decision to not go back to the place that caused you so much pain. What God wants to know is if you will trust Him in the middle of it? Will you seek Him first? Will you totally depend on Him?

I led the team for almost six years before I went to Pastor Murray and told him I needed to take a step down. This was probably one of the hardest decisions of my life. Jason and I are very active in ministry and sitting myself down was embarrassing and disappointing. I am supposed to be the strong one, the one people come to for answers and now my life is a complete mess. I was missing church, I wasn't leading as much anymore, I was delegating my responsibilities. Frankly, I was just there. I was wearing a mask, I was not whole, mentally, spiritually or emotionally and in order to lead people, you have to be whole.

On January 15, 2023, I sent the following message to each person on my Praise Team:

Jan 15, 2023 at 10:44 AM

I'm sharing this with you because you are an important person in my life. I value our relationship and trust that you will support me as I continue navigating this journey.

A little over 40 years ago, on Valentine's Day a new born baby was abandoned outside of MC Williams Middle School. I am "The BABY!" For my entire life, I have carried this burden, but I recognize now it's time for me to #ownmystory. In February, my story will air on ABC 13. I trust that you will continue to keep me in your thoughts & prayers. I love you & appreciate your support.

WOW!!!! You definitely have my prayers and support in EVERYTHING!!!!!

Text conversation with Praise Team

The amount of support I received thereafter was overwhelming. Although I knew they were there for me, I guess I just wasn't ready to share and have to answer questions. This was a part of my truth that I truly wanted to forget. Telling the story over and over was way too much, but the story was going to be airing soon on Channel 13, and I didn't want anyone to be surprised. As the song goes, "There are just some battles flesh and blood can't win, there'll be some moments that just don't make sense," and this was definitely one of those moments. It was a God Problem that only he could solve.

Through this journey, however, I had to start being kind to myself. It took me a while to forgive myself, to grant myself grace. Why am I forcing myself to uncover this information? I didn't do anything. Well, I did, I lived my entire life embarrassed by the hand I was dealt. I was ashamed. It felt as though I was practically living a lie.

Jeremiah 29:11 states: "'For I know the plans I have for you,' declares the Lord, 'plans to prosper you and not to harm you, plans to give you hope and a future.'" This has become one of my favorite scriptures.

He knew me before my mom and dad got together. He knew the decision she was going to make before she made it. Notice, I said, the decision "she" made.

My family in Louisiana didn't know I existed. She robbed us of the opportunity to know each other or at least would have if I never pursued the truth.

She made the choice and didn't consider the impact it would have on me or anyone else.

I was made in the image of God. Blessed be the God and Father of our Lord Jesus Christ, who has blessed us in Christ with every spiritual blessing in the heavenly places, even as he chose us in him before the foundation of the world, that we should be holy and blameless before him.

CHAPTER 17
CLEAN SLATE
"Clean" by Natalie Grant

T he reason we live the way we live is because of the way we think. I can't imagine the amount of guilt & pain that Dee has endured her entire life. Maybe this is why she was still so afraid to tell the whole truth even after confessing. Maybe she is afraid to reveal the entire story because she has been living in fear of it her entire life.

I always think about the day she abandoned her baby behind the school. I imagine carrying a baby to full term; feeling a baby kick, move, flutter, and then leaving it to die. As a mother, I can't fathom how someone could hurt their child so profoundly.

It reminds me of a devotional Joyce Meyer has called *"Closer to God Each Day. Quick to Forgive."* The title itself will set you free. In it, Joyce says, "The Bible teaches us to forgive 'readily and freely.' That is God's standard for us, no matter how we feel about it. We are to be quick to forgive.'"

I cite Joyce Meyer's devotionals because they are one of the special tools I used to survive my depression. I read a lot of devotionals during my journey through depression. I hope by sharing them it will help someone out there find the peace they seek.

According to 1 Peter 5:5, we are to clothe ourselves with the character of Jesus Christ, meaning we must choose to be long-suffering, patient, not easily offended, slow to anger, filled with mercy, and quick to forgive. No matter what has been done to you, remember, be quick to forgive.

My definition of mercy is to look beyond what is done to me that hurts and discover the reason why it was done. Many times, people do things even they don't understand, but there is always a reason why people behave the way they do. Perhaps they are hurting and in their own pain they don't even realize they are hurting someone else.

Understand God forgives! We are to be merciful and forgiving, just as God in Christ forgives us our trespasses. He not only sees what we do that is wrong, but He understands why we did it and is merciful and long-suffering.

The choice to forgive others is yours. God will not force you to do it. You must choose the path He offers. Even if you don't understand it, you must believe that God's way is the best. That's how it works.

And it does.

It works. I am proof. I am proof he can take what Satan intended to use to destroy you and turn it for your good.

Because of God, I understood I needed to give her a clean slate. Because of God, I knew I needed to give her a chance for us to start over. Well, not start over, but to start.

Because of God, I knew I needed to forgive her. Because of God, I recognized I needed to help her realize that her past doesn't define her. This is a brutal misunderstanding she must have lived with since she abandoned me; that her behavior that day defines her forever. It does not.

The power to decide what defines her is in her hands. God tells us we are to forgive in order to keep Satan from getting the advantage over us. Don't ever forget, this includes forgiving ourselves as well.

Today, I am a proud public educator and have been in education for approximately twenty years. I have an undergraduate degree from The University of Houston-Downtown, and a master's from Texas Southern University.

I am currently ABD; all but dissertation. This means I've done everything to complete my doctorate except passing a comprehensive exam and writing and defending my dissertation.

I was disappointed by this at first. I was struggling, in the beginning, watching my colleagues start and finish their programs.

It's okay, though! I was able to be there for them; to be present and celebrate their successes. I am the type of person who wants everyone to win, and my colleagues were winning their battles. This, however, didn't negate the fact that I felt defeated and unaccomplished.

I had a plan and life wasn't going accordingly. My goal was to become Dr. Leigha Curry before I turned forty years old, but it wasn't in the cards for me. I kept hitting roadblocks. Life wouldn't stop life-ing, but I gave it up to God, and the rest is history.

Such is the nature of success. The further we travel, the more obstacles we must hurdle.

Happily, this has not kept me from being a teacher, teacher coach, technology teacher, Teacher Specialist, Principal. School Support Officer, and currently a Senior Executive Director

When I think of the irony of it all, I am overwhelmed. I was abandoned behind a school, and I ended up dedicating my life to education. I must confess though, I strongly believe that it isn't so much irony as it is God's plan, from the back of the school to the front of the classroom. Maybe that's book number two?

If I can convey a moral to you it would be to believe in yourself. There's only one person you have to live with for the rest of your life, and that's you. Believe in that person. Believe in you. Your journey starts there.

EPILOGUE
MOVING FORWARD

"I'm Alive" by Rich Tolbert Jr.

A s I close this chapter of my life, I still have a million questions for Dee! Heck, get comfortable and I'll read to you from my list.

For starters, I want to know:

1. How has your life been since the time of my abandonment?

2. What significant events have happened?

3. Who helped you deliver me?

4. Did your mom know?

5. Did you know you were pregnant?

6. If so, how could you feel me move and kick and leave me to die?

7. What are your hopes for our relationship moving forward?

8. How do you envision our relationship developing over time?

9. Was there a specific situation or reason that led to the decision to abandon me?

These are just the first few questions right off the top. Sometimes I convince myself I will never get all the answers, and that makes me feel powerless. And yes, I still get angry, especially when getting answers begins to feel hopeless.

And then I am reminded . . .

When I feel certain of an outcome, I am reminded of the time when Dee said, "I thought I was going to take this to my grave." She had every reason to believe a newborn baby could not have survived that brutal day in 1982. She had every reason to believe none, but her confidants knew of her transgression. She had every reason to believe her secret would remain forever. And yet I survived. And I found her. Some forty years later, her past caught up to her.

It reminds me that what we believe to be certain is not necessarily certain *at all*. It reminds me that even when we have a very good reason to believe something, it might not be true, and we might not learn the truth until much later in life (if ever!). It reminds me that our construct of perception is fashioned heavily from pieces of misperception.

Knowing this has helped me take greater control over my outlook on life. If what we believe is only partial truth based on our limited perception, if our reality is ours to mold, then I chose to create positivity wherever I can.

I mean, how can I be whole if I am holding on to pain, hurt, and guilt? God never said the road would be easy. What He said was, "Be strong and courageous. Do not fear or be in dread of them, for it is the Lord your God who goes with you. He will not leave you or forsake you." (Deuteronomy 31:6). And He said, "I have said these things to you, that in me you may have peace. In the world you will have tribulation. But take heart; I have overcome the world." (John 16:33).

Every day I make an active conscious decision not to allow feelings of rejection, abandonment, and disappointment take over. Been there, done that. I wasn't my best self—not for me, my family, or anyone who depended on me. I have had to let the hurt and rejection from Dee and everyone else who was involved, go! Let it go! After all, I'm alive.

To Lillian Graham

"Grandmother, I think I found my biological mom," I said.

In the sweetest, most angelic voice she could muster, she replied, "She should be very proud of you. Keep praying for her. We don't know why she did what she did, but you are a blessing, the blessing in the blanket, my little angel."

My sweet Golden Girl died on Christmas Eve, December 24, 2024. A snapshot etched in my heart. A memory I will never forget. I can almost smell the light scent of White Diamonds as I type. I remember screaming over her cold body, saying, "You didn't get to read my book!" as the paramedics tried to usher me out. I was immovable. I was in a fog. I couldn't believe she was gone. My brother, Michael, picked me up from the floor and just comforted me.

Every day, every moment with her was one of love, comfort, and warmth. You couldn't help but be drawn to the sheer essence of who she was. In loving memory of my grandmother, Lillian Graham, she was a Life Master Bridge Player, a very distinguished honor considering the complexity of the game. Not only a master of the card game of Bridge, but a master builder in life. She bridged relationships, connections, and taught us valuable lessons of strategy, patience, and trust. Through her love of the game, she was a reflection of love and connection for her family. Her memory remains a cherished blessing, a reminder of the unwavering love and support she offered so freely. You are deeply missed but never forgotten.

Forever in my heart,
Leigha Curry, Your Lil Angel,
Your Blessing in the Blanket

www.ingramcontent.com/pod-product-compliance
Lightning Source LLC
Chambersburg PA
CBHW051314120626
46547CB00015B/2232